THE
HEART OF WALES
LINE TRAIL

**A wonderful walk weaving its way between stations
on one of Britain's most scenic railways
The route, from Craven Arms to Llanelli, is
227 km (141 miles)**

Les Lumsdon

KITTIWAKE

About the author

Les Lumsdon has written several books in the Kittiwake range. He has had a career in researching transport and tourism and is currently Professor Emeritus at the University of Central Lancashire. Les is a supporter of Rail Rambles (Mid Wales & The Marches) and enjoys using public transport to access walks. He lives near Ludlow in the Welsh Marches.

Published by **Kittiwake Books Limited**
3 Glantwymyn Village Workshops, Glantwymyn, Machynlleth,
Montgomeryshire SY20 8LY

© Text & map research: Les Lumsdon 2019

© Maps: Kittiwake Books Limited 2019

We are grateful to Stephen Miles, Geraint Morgan, Les Lumsdon and HoWLTA for supplying the cover photographs.

Care has been taken to be accurate.
However neither the author nor the publisher can accept responsibility for any errors which may appear, or their consequences.
If you are in any doubt about access, check before you proceed.

Printed by. Mixam UK

ISBN: 978 1 908748 57 7

Contents

The Upper Lugg Valley

INTRODUCTION

The Heart of Wales Line Trail describes a wonderful walk which weaves its way between stations on one of Britain's most scenic railways. The line from Shrewsbury to Swansea is 195 km (121 miles) long, passing through some of the least populated parts of Wales in a little over four hours. By contrast, the trail is over 227 km (141 miles) in length and might well take a walker 10 days to complete. It is eminently suitable for people looking for a long distance challenge and also for those who wish to walk the trail in sections, using the train to access day or weekend walking. Above all else it is spot on for those seeking to discover at first hand the beauty and tranquillity of the Welsh Marches and Mid Wales.

The trail starts off gently enough, but soon rises to remote uplands, dips into wooded valleys, and eventually passes alongside the captivating salt marshes of the Loughor Valley. The last leg takes you to the Millennium Coastal Park and final destination Llanelli, a town rightly proud of its industrial heritage. The appeal, of course, is not just the walking but also the train journey. It is one of the slowest trains in Wales, but do not let this put you off for this is not your everyday sort of train. This is a very rural line which defied closure during the Beeching era of the early 1960s. It ran through so many marginal seats that the line was given a reprieve; no one wanted to be responsible for pinning up that final closure notice. For those without a car it is a lifeline. For many it is simply irreplaceable. We are fortunate too, for it also happens to offer access to great walking between stations through pockets of landscape which are very different. In my book this is a marriage made in heaven.

Trail in the making

The trail has been the dream of many a walker for more years than I can recall, but as is often the case, a nudge is required to make it happen. This came about in 2015 when the Heart of Wales Line Development Company and Heart of Wales Line Travellers' Association decided to fuel that dream. Financial support to get it off the ground was provided by the then franchise holder, Arriva Trains Wales, and a feasibility study published in 2016 gave the project a green light. From then onwards it became a truly grassroots initiative helped along by the Development Company.

The implementation of the trail was kick started by pioneer supporters who put their hands in their pockets. It was topped up with small grants and a lot of work in kind and I mean a lot of work. At first, the trail team decided to call it "A trail in the making", working with cash strapped local authorities to make it happen. It is no longer in the making. Three years on it is up and running, ready for you to walk. Do not expect it to be manicured, there will always be trees down and wet ground to encounter, but together we'll keep on improving it. Needless to say, I hope that you enjoy every step of the way as much as we have enjoyed developing it.

The Route

The trail starts in Craven Arms, a small town which owes its existence to the railway, and soon heads to the rolling landscape of South Shropshire on its route to the seashore of South Wales. The Shropshire Hills provide one of the loveliest landscapes in the Welsh Marches. The area is farmed, but with so many artisans as well as farmworkers making a living hereabouts, all summer there are shows, open days and village events where they exhibit their wares and serve up locally grown food.

There's something very appealing about the lush river valleys too. Perhaps it is the dappled waters shaded by alders which were once cropped to make clogs. These water meadows are interspersed with the pockets of rough ground and thickets where wildlife thrives. The meadows give way to enclosed grass green slopes rising to wooded hilltops, hunting grounds of the ancients. At one time crowned with wild wood, they are now more than often dominated by coniferous canopies albeit with a veneer of deciduous woodland to keep us recreationalists happy.

Sentinels of the past

Immortalised in Housman's poetry as a one of the quietest places under the sun, the Shropshire Hills Area of Outstanding Natural Beauty makes a good introduction to the Welsh Marches, that indeterminate area which straddles the border of England and Wales. It has not always been this tranquil. As you wander through what is now called Mortimer country, think on awhile. The Mortimers, and for that matter other Marcher lords, ruled the Marches with an iron fist and there are the scars to show for it. Castles and ancient farmsteads stand steadfast on the landscape here, and each with a story of woe to tell. There were not many happy endings. These historic sites, including a large number of hillforts, are the sentinels of the past, but so are veteran trees along the route many of which are well over 400 years old, often mark changes in landscape history such as enclosure boundaries, or cartways that no longer exist. They are marvellous survivors from a time gone by, as are yews to be found in the churchyards of border villages.

It is, of course an ever changing environment, sometimes offering promise for the future such as the River Clun Project which will hopefully restore river habitats and encourage the rare freshwater pearl mussel to thrive again. But as Iolo Williams, writer and TV presenter notes, the loss of habitat diversity is a pressing matter.

Imperceptibly into Wales

You might think you would slip imperceptibly into Wales by way of an old drovers' road, but there's a timely reminder of the age old partition, Offa's Dyke. This amazing linear monument is testament to the sheer power and determination of Offa, the King of Mercia over 1200 years ago, to provide a boundary which would stay. There are tangible remains of the earthworks and to a lesser extent the dyke, but needless to say your eyes will be drawn to the views which are simply superb. Look out for the Offa's Dyke Centre which provides both welcome refreshment and information.

For the most part the trail lies in Wales and hence the welcome, Croeso y Gymru at the border. The trail runs through Powys, which has witnessed little industrial development and its very rurality is one of the appeals of the route. It soon traverses the upland moors of old Radnorshire, once known as 'rugged Radnor', distant from the goings on of the world, where skylarks and meadow pipits can be heard if not seen and Red Kites circle above with endless ease. Grouse, merlin, and short eared owls frequent these remote hill tops too, but in limited numbers. These are the places where open views across the mountains of Mid Wales seem infinite, where walking is an experience and a westerly breeze freshens the day. But be warned, in winter this land can be harsh. Whatever the season, you'll certainly be able to see the rain coming in, so you need to be well prepared.

This high ground gives way to 'ffridd', where rough grassy patches, sometimes tussocky grass with wet flushes, dominate the landscape, often clothed in gorse, hawthorn, bracken and scrub, semi-wild places where sheep graze their summer days. These are the places where you're likely to see whinchats and wheatears in spring and fieldfares and redwings as winter approaches. These 'in between' patches of rougher, uncultivated ground are havens for wildlife.

Beautiful wooded valleys

For me the diversity offered by a succession of beautiful wooded valleys in this mid trail section, makes the walk especially appealing. Broad leaved woodlands dominate with ash and oak being favourite trees on the acid soils, but on the edges are underwood such as hazel and elder. Several are managed well to stop livestock and deer from grazing in excess and are refuge to a wide range of flora and fauna, contrasting sharply with the seemingly endless swathes of rye grass sheep pasture. But be assured, you'll not just come across any old sheep. Some will be rarer breeds which local farmers have nurtured over the centuries, the likes of Beulah Speckled Face, Hill Radnor and Kerry Hill.

To walk beneath canopies of native trees, lightened by shafts of soft summer sunshine, are moments to be treasured. The trail dips down to the sparkling waters of a river or tributary brook, maybe a trickle in summer, but in full-flow most of the time. There are rod fishing rivers too, spawning ground for grayling, trout and salmon and cherished by the fishing fraternity. It is hereabouts that you might catch sight of the kingfisher and dipper. Unfortunately, as pure as these rivers look, they are increasingly affected by run off.

Agriculture and forestry still reign supreme across most of the route, although in truth tourism is important to the economy and has been for 200 years or more. In the earliest days the pursuit of the 'Picturesque', a movement of early painters and writers with a particular focus on natural landscapes, gained momentum in the Welsh Marches. It also attracted the venturesome to travel to these parts in search of what is best described as a wild Wales. While we say natural and wild, it is often forgotten that for thousands of years humans had been shaping this 'wild' landscape.

Nevertheless, the observation of landforms in Mid Wales certainly became fashionable from the late 18th century onwards for those who could afford a carriage and servants. The likes of writers Pennant and Shelley, as well as painters such as Devis and Wilson encouraged others to make their way to Mid Wales and onward to Aberystwyth. Of course, the most romantic of them all George Borrow, an inveterate walker by the way, laid down an imprint of Welsh life in the 1850s when he penned his engaging book Wild Wales. This encouraged many other English authors to tread in his footsteps. Even the Cambrian Railways, perhaps a decade or so later, used the phrase Picturesque to entice urban masses to seek out destinations in deepest Wales on route to the coast.

Another form of tourism blossomed in Mid Wales too, an equally genteel pursuit, known as 'taking of the waters'. In the latter decades of the 18th century this fashionable pastime began to grow despite the poor state of most roads. The surge of interest by English writers led to the expansion of four spa towns, all of which are located on the trail- Llandrindod, Builth, Llangammarch and Llanwrtyd. They all took advantage of the Victorian bourgeoisie's desire for improved well-being. The momentum increased so much that they all changed their place name to include the word 'Wells'. The arrival of the train in the 1860s precipitated a boom and given continued overly-hyped press coverage, society notables flocked to these spa towns for decades to come. Unfortunately, the demand abated in the 1920s when people started to seek out seaside resorts instead. The spas are, for the most part, lost but there remains a legacy which encourages outdoor pursuits for the air is good in Powys.

Underrated county

The trail travels south to Carmarthenshire, an underrated county with a subtle mix of verdant woods and rolling foothills particularly around the old market towns of Llandovery and Llandeilo. Admittedly, there are more pockets of wet rush to contend with, but in return you are rewarded with exquisite views over to the Carmarthenshire Fans and, of course, there'll be time to admire that railway engineering masterpiece, Cynghordy viaduct. It also brings a chance to discover intriguing places such as Myddfai and Carn Goch located in the western fringe of the Brecon Beacons National Park; both providing different insights into Welsh culture. The Trail also runs by castle ruins at Llandovery and Castell Carreg Cennen, impressive structures built by the Normans determined to subjugate Welsh people, in turn who fought passionately to resist Anglo-Norman domination.

South of Llandeilo the landscape changes; it is pitted with old limestone quarries, works and kilns of industry which time has allowed nature to re-engage and to soften the scars. Further south again the legacy of coal mining and tinplate manufacture are less evident on the ground, but are nevertheless deeply ingrained in the culture of the

Amman and Loughor valleys where there were numerous collieries and associated industries from 19th century onwards. The intriguing sculpture by Bowcott, located in one of Ammanford's main streets, neatly encapsulates the importance of coal in the valley's history and the trail passes by this splendid sculpture.

The trail eases into the City and County of Swansea for the last section through to the seashore. Standing on the moorland of Graig Fawr, far above Pontarddulais, you could be a million miles away from it all, observing the serpent like shape of the Llwchwr Estuary and over to the Gower Peninsula. From this vantage point it is hard to believe that the area was once a hotbed of early industrial development, but within a mile or so there are remnants of quarries and pits and factories which produced coal, stone and tinplate for export throughout the world.

The final section follows the estuary down to the village of Loughor to join the Wales Coast Path. It is important to mention that there's also a braid on the western flank of the estuary via Llangennech. It's an alternative route, recommended when the tide is running high and floods the trail near Castell Ddu. Either way you reach Bynea, and the distance is the same. There is, at Loughor or Bynea, the option to follow the one of several routes through to Swansea. However, the trail joins the Coast Path westward to Llanelli passing by the Wetland Centre, an amazing place to discover wildlife in seashore wetlands. It then proceeds to the Millennium Coastal Park Discovery Centre at Llanelli, some 227 km (141 miles) from the Shropshire Hills Discovery Centre at Craven Arms.

There's one short final urban section which exhibits another dimension of Welsh culture, there being two fine examples of nonconformist chapels reflecting a time when religious fervour spread through South Wales. These chapels are described in detail by Huw Edwards (TV newsreader and author) in his meticulously researched tome, *Capeli Llanelli*. Edwards' work provides a captivating insight into a town that was once a major port and manufacturing centre. The chapels are located near to Llanelli railway station, journey's end on this remarkably diverse trail.

Walking the Trail

There's a main route which weaves its way between most communities served directly by the Heart of Wales Railway. Wherever possible we have routed the trail via stations, after all that's one of the key elements. There are 30 stations between Craven Arms and Llanelli, but unfortunately it does not pass by four of the rural halts, in some cases they are not served well by rights of ways. A classic example has to be the Sugar Loaf halt which has no public rights of way nearby. There are several cases, however, where there are station links to and from the main trail, often down back lanes or village paths to the nearest station. You'll find these very helpful in joining or leaving the trail at various locations. For example, the trail passes through the village of Hopton Castle, but the station is 2 km (1.2 miles) away, a lovely saunter along a lane to Hopton Heath Station. These are noted in the guide.

The trail is identified by a bespoke waymark which is used throughout on the main trail; a special station link roundel is used where there are links to stations. However, the Heart of Wales Line Trail joins several other routes including two national trails, Offa's Dyke Path and Glyndŵr's Way being the most notable. There are no Heart of Wales Line Trail markers on these sections and in some cases you will need to follow the trail marker of the respective regional or national trail where the Heart of Wales Line Trail shares a section. This is one of the highlights of the trail as it keeps company with the Shropshire Way, Offa's Dyke Trail, Glyndŵr's Way, Wye Valley Walk, Epynt Way, Beacons Way, St Illtyd's Walk and the Wales Coast Path.

Great Expectations

It is best to think of the trail as a work in progress. It is totally fresh and a great way of exploring the Marches and mid Wales, nothing less than inspirational in places. We have done our best to upgrade route infrastructure, working alongside each respective local authority. In some places, what is best described as regional trail standard (similar to the Wye Valley Walk or Beacons Way) has been achieved, but in other places there is still need for improvement. Therefore, please bear with us if there's a boardwalk missing or you find a stile where a small gate would be ideal. Our aim is to upgrade year on year and by using the route you are helping us to achieve this goal.

One of the charms of the trail is the number of wet meadows, common rush pastures and winterbourne streams which you'll encounter; these habitats are becoming rarer so we need to look after them. Having said that you can expect to get wet feet, for certain after heavy rain, and in some places there'll be more mud than you would like. Leggings and boots are essential unless it is a dry summer.

At the southern end of the trail there can be flooding in one section when there are high tides on the Llwchwr Estuary; check the tide table before walking between Pontarddulais and Loughor via Morfa Mawr. An alternative is offered via Llangennech and both braids are a similar distance and lead to Bynea where you continue on the Wales Coast Path.

If you come across a problem on any part of the trail, such as an obstruction, then please contact the respective local authority:

Shropshire: outdoor.recreation@shropshire.gov.uk
Powys: rightsofway@powys.gov.uk
Carmarthenshire: prowmaintenance@carmarthenshire.gov.uk
Swansea: countrysideaccess@swansea.gov.uk

Updates

These websites will be useful in planning your ramble:
Heart of Wales Line Trail: heartofwaleslinetrail.co.uk
National Rail Enquiries: www.nationalrail.co.uk
Local Buses: www.travel.cymru

Ramblers: www.ramblers.org.uk
Rail Rambles: www.railrambles.com
Walkers are Welcome: www.walkersarewelcome.com

Wildlife Trusts
Shropshire: www.shropshirewildlifetrust.org.uk
Radnorshire: www.rwtwales.org
South and West Wales: www.welshwildife.org

Thanks

Thanks go to the trail steering group founder members- Robin Barlow, Rachel Francis, John Maudsley, Mike Watson, Paul Salveson and more recently John Ashley-for their hard work in bringing the trail to fruition. I am also grateful to Alison Caffyn, the principal consultant who finalised the trail report, to the many individual walkers and Rambler' groups for testing sections of the trail and equally for the rights of way/countryside access teams in each respective local authority. Special thanks go to Rachel Francis and Pat Lumsdon for proof reading. If there are any mistakes or omissions that is down to me and I will do my best to rectify in due course.

The royalties from this book will be ploughed back into trail maintenance so a very big thanks to you for purchasing the guide.

Rail Ramblers at Bucknell

Heart of Wales Line Trail...Distance Checklist from station to station

	Location	km	mls
1	Craven Arms Stn to Broome Stn	8.5	5.3
2	Broome Stn to Bucknell Stn	17	10.6
3	Bucknell Stn to Knighton Stn	14	8.7
4	Knighton Stn to Knucklas Stn	7	4.3
5	Knucklas Stn to Llanbister Rd Stn	18	8.3
6	Llanbister Rd stn to Pen-y-bont Stn	17	10.2
7	Pen-y-bont stn to Llandrindod Stn	11	6.9
8	Llandrindod Stn to Builth Wells (Groe)	25	15.5
9	Builth Wells (Groe) to Llanwrtyd Stn	22.5	14
10	Llanwrtyd Stn to Cynghordy Stn	18	11
11	Cynghordy Stn to Llandovery Stn	11	6.8
12	Llandovery Stn to Llangadog Stn	19	11.8
13	Llangadog Stn to Llandeilo Stn	16	10
14	Llandeilo Stn to Ammanford Stn	19	11.8
15	Ammanford Stn to Pontarddulais Stn	14	8.7
16	Pontarddulais Stn to Llanelli Stn	20	12

Please note that this includes links to and from some stations and some rounding; the sum of the distances are therefore greater than the main route which is 227 km (141 miles)

Ordnance Survey Explorer Maps covering the trail

217	The Long Mynd & Wenlock Edge
201	Knighton & Presteigne
214	Llanidloes & Newtown
200	Llandrindod Wells & Elan Valley
188	Builth Wells
187	Llandovery
OL12	Brecon Beacons National Park (western area)
186	Llandeilo & Brecha Forest
178	Llanelli & Ammanford

1 CRAVEN ARMS STATION TO BROOME STATION

8.5 km (5.3 miles)

This is it, the start. Take a brisk walk through the streets of Craven Arms to the Shropshire Hills Discovery Centre, a necessary pit stop for refreshment and information, then head off west through the rolling landscape of the South Shropshire Hills, through the ancient parish of Sibdon Carwood, over Hopesay Common into the Clun Valley at Aston-on-Clun.

The trail follows the black town fingerposts through to the Discovery Centre. Leave Craven Arms Railway Station from Platform 2 into the station car park and turn almost immediately right along a narrow urban path, signed to Town Centre, which runs between gardens and fencing. Go left at the junction, by the higher security fencing, then cut right across the supermarket car park to the main A49 road. Cross the main road with great care and turn right to reach Corvedale Road (B4368) running left from a mini roundabout. Walk along this main street until you reach Market Street on the right, take this turn and walk straight ahead, past the Land of Lost Content Nostalgia Museum and vintage shops until you reach the Stokesay Inn. Go left to the entrance of the Shropshire Hills Discovery Centre, an alternative starting point.

Craven Arms grew from not much more than a cluster of houses into a railway town in the 19th century. It is hard to imagine how extensive the station was in the late 19th century. It was opened on the 20th April, 1852, and railway sidings were added soon after to allow the transhipment of all manner of agricultural goods – sheep, cattle, bags of grain and clover as well as skins for tanning. There used to be an old wooden station board which adorned the platform for decades; it advised passengers that Craven Arms and Stokesay Station was

the junction for the Central Wales Route to Llandrindod, Brecon, Llanelly, Swansea, Carmarthen, Tenby and Pembroke Dock. All of these destinations are still possible, although passengers for Brecon will have to change at Llandrindod for the T5 bus. Sadly Craven Arms Station is now in a minimal state but you never know.

The Shropshire Hills Discovery Centre, housed in an unusual looking building with a grass roof designed to reflect the shape of an ancient hillfort, is a major attraction in South Shropshire. It includes an exhibition, café and shop open daily from 10 until 5. Managed by the charity Grow Cook and Learn, it has a mission to connect people to the food, history and landscape of the Shropshire Hills...a great place to start your walk.

2 If starting at the Shropshire Hills Discovery Centre, leave via the main entrance, through the car park, step over the road and turn left. Cross the A49 at the pedestrian crossing, go left and immediately right along a path into Dodds Lane. Keep ahead to join a track; this runs beneath the Marches railway line to a stile by a gate. Enter the field and head slightly right following the line of several old trees. Cross a stile and head slightly right towards the hedge alongside the Heart of Wales railway. Go ahead, making your way over three stiles as you walk through fields to Park Lane.

3 Turn right here, under the railway to the B4368. Cross with care over to a dead end road and then ahead to join Watling Street – *a Roman road which linked Viroconium (Wroxeter) to Isca Silurian (Caerleon).* Go left on a path at a finger post showing the Shropshire Way, passing several new dwellings, to a kissing gate leading into a field. Proceed ahead over three stiles at field boundaries. Look for a gateway and stile on the left nearly mid-way up the next field. Go through here and head slightly right, aiming for a waymark post and small footbridge, then across to a stile which leads into a lane. Beware of traffic before you cross.

4 Go through a kissing gate directly opposite into parkland. Head slightly left by the waymark post. *You'll see the buildings of 17th century Sibdon Castle built by the Corbet family and 12th century Sibdon Carwood church (although it was much altered in the 1740s) over to the right.* Go through a kissing gate, over a carriage drive, and through two more gates, over a footbridge and gate to enter a large parkland pasture. Now aim very slightly right; mid-way there's a waymark post under a second large oak tree. From here aim to the left of a stone cottage seen ahead, where you cross a stile a few metres beyond.

5 Rise up on a track into a pasture just to the left of a hedge and follow the hedge line for about 100 metres before easing slightly left up the field to a gate marked by tall Scots pines just beyond. Head left up a track to follow the woodland boundary all the way round to the far bottom left corner of the field, where you pass to the left of a ruined building: the ground is often wet near here. Rise up to step over a stile and continue along a fence to a junction of footpaths marked by a fingerpost.

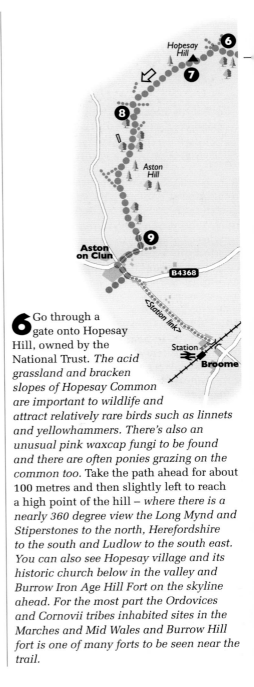

6 Go through a gate onto Hopesay Hill, owned by the National Trust. *The acid grassland and bracken slopes of Hopesay Common are important to wildlife and attract relatively rare birds such as linnets and yellowhammers. There's also an unusual pink waxcap fungi to be found and there are often ponies grazing on the common too.* Take the path ahead for about 100 metres and then slightly left to reach a high point of the hill – *where there is a nearly 360 degree view the Long Mynd and Stiperstones to the north, Herefordshire to the south and Ludlow to the south east. You can also see Hopesay village and its historic church below in the valley and Burrow Iron Age Hill Fort on the skyline ahead. For the most part the Ordovices and Cornovii tribes inhabited sites in the Marches and Mid Wales and Burrow Hill fort is one of many forts to be seen near the trail.*

9 Once through, go ahead on a lane which bends right to drop down to Aston on Clun and in the centre of the village, the Arbor Tree, for which Aston

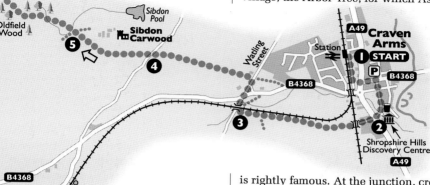

is rightly famous. At the junction, cross over the B4368 road with care and turn left to walk along the pavement to Redwood Drive. Ahead is the Kangaroo Inn and just a few metres further on and down the lane to the right (B4369 to Broome) is the Community Shop where tea and coffee is available.

*N**ear to the Arbor Tree** is an interpretation case which tells the charming story of how the villagers decorate a black poplar tree every year, partly to retain the celebration first ordered by King Charles II in 1660, but also to commemorate the marriage of Squire Marston to Mary Carter of Sibdon Carwood in 1786. There are also round houses in the village dating from the late 18th century which are said to have been built by a local character at the time. In all of the villages there are half-timbered cottages, buildings which used timber frames filled in with wattle and daub or brick were often preferred to the use of stone in the Marches.*

Station Link

At Aston on Clun you can link to Broome station by continuing along the B4369, past the Community Shop to Broome railway station, which is a further half a kilometre down this lane. The entrance to the railway station is on the

7 Keep ahead to the left of a clump of tall trees and down the hill aiming to the right of a large house in the valley. In the bottom corner of the common slip through the kissing gate to leave the Shropshire Way, and turn left to drop down to a kissing gate and a drive, passing a dwelling on the right. Cross over and go through a small gate and over a footbridge. The path leads slightly right through the woodland to exit over another stile into a pasture.

8 Continue slightly to the right towards a waymark post; the path bends right and left to another stile. Proceed through another small wood, keeping ahead alongside a fence to your left to reach another pasture. The path passes by gorse and scrub as you continue ahead to follow a grass track beneath a bank of gorse. There are several waymark posts to guide you and then the track runs beneath cottages and down to a field gate.

right before the bridge. Unfortunately, the Engine & Tender pub, a popular local at one time, is currently closed.

Refreshments and Accommodation

Craven Arms: shops, cafes, restaurants and pubs plus a range of accommodation

Aston-on-Clun: community shop serving tea and

coffee, Kangaroo Inn

Bus and Train

Buses from Shrewsbury to Ludlow call at Craven Arms, service 435

Twice weekly bus from Ludlow and Craven Arms to Aston-on-Clun, service 745

Railway halt at Broome

2 BROOME STATION TO BUCKNELL STATION

17 km (10.6 miles) with cut off at Hopton Heath after 8km (5 miles)

The trail makes its way through the Clun Valley to the village of Clunbury nestled beneath a rather impressive Clunbury Hill, denuded of most of its woodland, except for a prominent group of trees seen for miles around. The trail then rises over a watershed to the small village of Hopton Castle where a visit to the castle is a must. There's now some climbing to do in earnest as you make your way through Hopton Wood to Meeroak before descending into the Redlake Valley. There are splendid views down into the valley and the final stretch follows a woodland path above the flowing waters of the Redlake, a tributary of the Clun, both of which are habitats for endangered freshwater pearl mussels.

I See instruction at the end of the last section for the link from Broome to Aston on Clun, past the community shop entrance and by the Kangaroo Inn. Walk down Redwood Drive, ignoring the junction on the right, to reach a track, slightly right, just beyond the houses. The path cuts right before a gate. Follow the path as it bends left and through two gates and temporary sheep pens to enter a field. You'll see a stile ahead and one over in a fence on the right. Cross the stile on the right into the large field, then keep ahead, parallel to a line of old trees to a kissing gate in the hedge; this leads onto a lane.

2 Go left to wander along to a bridge over the rippling waters of the River Clun into the hamlet of Beambridge and turn right. Follow this lane for less than a kilometre in the shadow of Clunbury hill which was covered in oak in medieval times, an integral part of the wider Clun

hunting forest. As the road bends slightly left under a canopy of trees you cut right down to a footbridge over the River Clun which is visible from the road above.

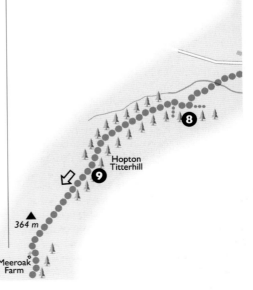

Hopton Titterhill

364 m

Meeroak Farm

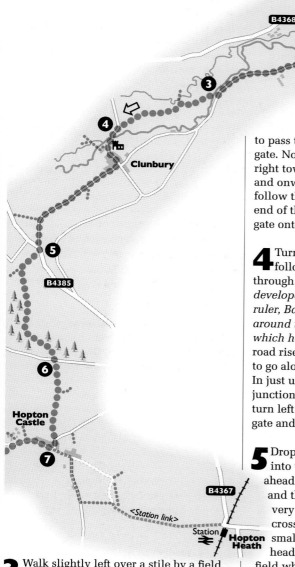

to pass through another gate. Now head very slightly right towards an old oak tree and onward to a field gate. Once through, follow the hedge to your right and at the end of the field go through another field gate onto a road.

4 Turn left to walk over the bridge, following the road which winds through the pretty village of Clunbury, *developed in medieval times by a Norman ruler, Baron de Say. The village is nestled around the church dedicated to St Withins which has a fine 12th century nave.* The road rises up to a junction; bear right here to go along a lane signposted to Twitchen. In just under a kilometre you reach a junction with the B4385. Cross with care turn left to a walk 50 metres to a kissing gate and go through it.

5 Drop down to walk over a small bridge into the next field. Aim for the barn ahead and at the waymark post cut left and then right to skirt the barn (often very muddy here) then slightly right to cross over a ditch before you reach a small gate in the hedge. Go through and head very slightly right to the top of the field where you cross a double stile. Rise up alongside the wood on the right then head across the pasture to a stile leading into woodland, not easily seen in summer. Cross this and within a few metres to the right, the path heads leftwards and climbs gradually up a bank to a waymark post at a

3 Walk slightly left over a stile by a field gate. Follow a line of trees just to your right and over another stile by a gate. Continue ahead to pass near a dwelling seen on the right; aim just to the right of a small barn where you cross a stile by a field gate. Walk alongside a line of hazels

forestry track. Go left and proceed for about 250 metres, looking out just before the descent, for a path on the right. Follow this through the wood up to a kissing gate at a country lane.

*H*opton Castle *dates from the 14th century, but is remembered for an atrocity carried out in the English Civil War when the castle was besieged by Royalists. The Parliamentarians, under the command of Samuel More, refused to surrender despite the odds being stacked heavily against them and thus snubbed customary practice. This rattled the Royalists and when the Parliamentarians finally succumbed they were slaughtered in a brutal fashion and from that day commentators have referred to Hopton Castle as being the byword for treachery.*

6 Go over the lane, cross a stile and follow the right hand edge of the field where there are good views ahead towards Wales. Cross a stile into the next field and you will see the ruins of Hopton Castle below. Head slightly right; you are aiming for a point just to the left of a derelict building. Go over the stile and a track dips down to a drive and then a lane. Keep ahead to a junction at Hopton Castle. If continuing to Bucknell turn right.

Station Link

At this point it is possible to follow a link path for a mile 1.5 km (just under a mile) to Hopton Heath Station passing by Hopton Castle. Go left along the road and turn first right signposted to Bedstone. The castle is on the right (free entry). Pass a dwelling and look for a stile on the left. Cross this and head over the field to a field gate and bridge over a stream. Walk slightly right, go through another field gate onto a lane, and turn right to walk along the lane into Hopton Heath. At the junction keep right across the railway bridge then walk down steps to the platform.

7 Walk through the village with the small stream to your left; the church of St Edward is across a field to the right as the road bends left to pass the entrance of Upper House Farm. As it rises and begins to ease right, go through a gate into a field and follow the tractor track ahead, through two pastures and gates. The track rises, bends right and then left to reach a field gate into Hopton Wood, managed by the Forestry Commission

8 Go left up to a junction and turn sharp right onto a woodland track, sometimes shared with bicycles as there are some mountain bike trails at Hopton. Follow this track round gentle bends until it starts to descend, where at a waymark post, you cut left upwards on a track which climbs steadily for some distance, passing one waymark post at a junction before reaching the top.

9 Cross straight over the forestry track and continue ahead on a grassy footpath. Where the track veers left following the conifers, go straight ahead, passing on your left a conifer seed nursery; the path can be a little overgrown in summer. Eventually, you reach a small gate before Meeroak Farm. Go through and head to the left of a barn. Follow the track through gates and down to a drive. Continue ahead until you go through a gateway. Turn right here, along the edge of a wood, and when the path looks to cut left, the right of way is actually on the right over a stile into a field.

10 Go slightly right across the field to the opposite boundary by the wood. Turn right here to walk down the field edge to cross a stile by a gate; *you are rewarded by wonderful views up the Redlake Valley.* Continue down over another stile by a gate, past Honeyhole Farm. Follow the hedge to the left down towards a kissing gate above

18

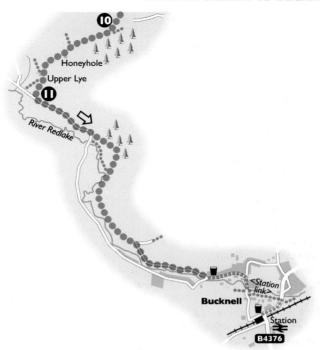

a house and stables. Go through the kissing gate and keep to the left hand boundary through the garden to a metal field gate on the left. Follow as waymarked through the gate into the field, turn right down the field following the hedge on the right to exit at a gate onto the road.

Go left. Where the road bends sharply right, go through the gate on your left. Head slightly right and along the track uphill, through a gate and past a line of redwoods. On reaching another field gate ease off right along a bridleway; it contours round the base of Bucknell Hill, through woodland. After you leave the woodland pass through a gate and at the next boundary a field gate into Bridgend Lane, towards the centre of Bucknell where you emerge on to the main road. If you are continuing on the trail turn right at the end of Bridgend Lane.

Station Link

Turn left for the railway station, past the Baron Inn. The road bends right and across a bridge. Turn left after the bridge, along a surfaced path to the left of the parish church. This gives out at another main road. Turn right to pass the Sitwell Arms, and over the level crossing to enter the station.

Refreshments and Accommodation

Hopton Heath: accommodation
Bucknell: post office and two shops, Baron and Sitwell Arms public houses
Accommodation available

Bus and Train

Buses from Ludlow to knighton via Hopton Heath and Bucknell, service 738/740
Railway halts at Hopton Heath (station link to Hopton Castle), Bucknell

3 BUCKNELL STATION TO KNIGHTON (Tref-y-Clawdd)

14 km (8.7 miles)

From here, the terrain changes as you climb through Bucknell Wood to join an old drovers' road across higher ground above the Redlake Valley. You'll catch sight of the Iron Age hillfort Caer Caradoc above the village of Chapel Lawn as well as distant view back to the Long Mynd and another Caer Caradoc camp above Church Stretton. The trail continues through sheep pastures to Offa's Dyke Path and onward to Knighton. There are exceptional views across Mid-Wales from here.

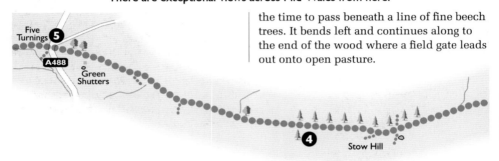

the time to pass beneath a line of fine beech trees. It bends left and continues along to the end of the wood where a field gate leads out onto open pasture.

Station Link

From Bucknell station, see information provided at the end of the last section.

1 Go right to continue west on the lane in Bucknell and over a small bridge. At the right hand bend keep straight ahead into Daffodil Lane passing by recreational grounds. The lane begins to rise; keep ahead at the fork onto a track.

2 The track continues to rise to a junction then levels before reaching a second junction in Bucknell Wood. Go right here to join a forestry track and, stay on this as it climbs up and bends to the right. At the second fork, take the left hand track upwards. The track curves further left and rises again through a group of native trees, principally oaks. Eventually, you reach a staggered junction; go left and then follow the track as it curves right, climbing all of

3 The route continues westwards for some miles now along an old drovers' road until it reaches Offa's Dyke Path. Follow the tractor track ahead *from which there are fine views across to Caer Caradoc hillfort sitting above the hamlet of Chapel Lawn, nestled below in the Upper Redlake valley. There are also views back to the other Caer Caradoc near Church Stretton, to the Wrekin and Clee Hills.* At the junction of tracks, keep ahead through a gate and walk up to the wood at Stowe Hill. Go through another field gate and pass by a stile on the right.

4 Continue ahead to go through two gates by a belt of woodland. Follow the track ahead through a number of pastures passing through four field gates. The track becomes enclosed by hedges and is wet in places as it descends through another gate

Ducks on the River Redlake

Follow the fence on the left hand side to proceed through a small gate and ahead along a green track to a gate; just beyond, the bridleway crosses the Offa's Dyke Path National Trail.

and by buildings to reach the main road at Five Turnings. *This literally describes the name of the hamlet nestled around a junction of five roadways.*

5 Cross the main road with extreme care and go through a small gate just behind the GR post box to continue on the drovers' route between hedges and then go through a gate and slightly left rising up a large field towards pine trees on the ridge ahead.

O *ffa's Dyke was undoubtedly an expensive form of early border control. Built by Offa, the King of Mercia, over a period from 757 to 796, this large mound some 6 metres high and with ditches to match was certainly defensive in nature, but probably also had a softer function as a point for the exchange of goods and services. Although not continuous between Prestatyn and Chepstow there's approximately 80 miles of monument* *remaining and Offa's Dyke Path is the only way to explore at close quarters.*

6 However, you turn left to follow the national trail (waymarked with acorn symbols) through to Knighton. *There's a good example of the ancient monument just to your left; it is hard to believe that the path actually ran along the monument here in previous decades.* Make your way ahead, passing through several gates always with a fence to the left. *There are magnificent views up the Teme Valley and across to Knucklas Castle, village and railway viaduct.* On reaching a seat at a local viewpoint at Panpwnton Hill, the path curves left to become narrower as it drops down the hillside to a finger post. Go right here to drop steeply down to a lane, so neat footwork is required as the path is heavily eroded in places.

Station Link

Those needing to walk directly to Knighton railway station should cut left here along the lane; it is about 20 minutes brisk walk from here to the station. Those joining the trail from Knighton Railway see the next section.

7 .Cross the lane, go through a gate and follow the worn path to cross the railway track and bridge spanning the Rive Teme. Follow the river bank as it curves to the left, through kissing gates into woodland where you cross the England – Wales border. The path rises and turns right up to the Offa's Dyke Centre and Knighton town centre.

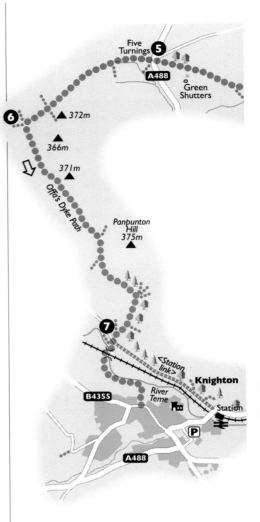

Refreshments and Accommodation

Chapel Lawn: accommodation, one kilometre from the route at Stowe Hill

Knighton: shops, cafés, restaurants and pubs plus a range of accommodation

Bus and Train

Buses from Kington to Knighton, service 41
Buses from Ludlow to Knighton, service 738/740
Railway halt at Bucknell and station at Knighton

4 KNIGHTON STATION TO KNUCKLAS STATION

7 km (4.4 miles)

This short section rises above the town to Knighton's old racecourse before descending to the enterprising community of Knucklas (Cnwclas), nestled beneath the remains of a Norman castle built to rule over the people of the Teme Valley. There are exceptionally good views of the railway viaduct and the Heyop valley as you drop down into the village.

1 Leave Knighton Railway Station to walk up Station Road, passing the Horse and Jockey pub to a junction with the Knighton Hotel opposite. Go right into Broad Street to rise up to the Clock Tower. *Those coming in from the Offa's Dyke Discovery Centre need to turn left from the entrance of the centre to walk along West Street to the Clock Tower. From here you will be following Glyndŵr's Way out of town to Rookery Lane; this is a national trail so you will need to follow the Acorn trail waymarks.*

Knighton *is well known to walkers making their way on Offa's Dyke Path. Its Welsh name, Tref-y-Clawdd, literally means town on the dyke. In so many respects it is the archetypal border town, standing above the River Teme and watered by the Wylcwm brook. It is no wonder that the Normans were keen to secure the valley at this point. They built a fortress at the top of the town (it is not possible to access any remaining earthworks) and another at Bryn-y-Castell, east of the cattle market above the Community Hall. They clearly could not make their minds up as to which would hold out best against the Welsh. That is understandable, the castles changed hands a fair number of times. The fierce Welsh incursions often required a rebuilding of town walls, as well as buildings and the castles. However, it was not the only reason; several Norman lordships fell out with successive kings and they were soon removed by the monarchy. The medieval period was a troublesome time for Knighton folk.*

The town has always served as a market for agricultural goods, certainly from the 13th century onwards as it was granted a charter in 1230. It was also as a stop off for drovers and a staging point on coach routes before the arrival of the train in 1861. Evidently, the latter gave a boost to trade unparalleled since the 1840s. In recent decades Knighton has engaged in tourism. It is a Walkers Are Welcome town and the Offa's Dyke Centre (managed by the Offa's Dyke Association) houses a superb exhibition as well as an information centre and café.

2 From the Clock Tower head up High Street leading into The Narrows, a steep pedestrian thoroughfare. This rises up to a junction just beyond the Golden Lion pub in Castle Road, a clue that the old earthworks are nearby, but unfortunately hidden by development. Go left here and in approximately 100 metres keep right. Just beyond the junction with Plough Road, descend a paved path on the left to cross Mill Road and drop down again to George Road. Keep right here to walk between cottages and waterside gardens. Continue ahead on a surfaced path near to the Wylcwm brook. This rises up to Mill Road. Cross over and climb by gardens and

23

pass the end of a drive. Cross the wider Penybont Road and proceed up a drive, but cut right to climb again by gardens up to Garth Lane.

Glyndŵr's Way *is one of the three National Trails in Wales. It is 217 km (135 miles) in length running from Knighton to Machynlleth and back to Welshpool. It commemorates Owain Glyndŵr, the last native Welsh person to be Prince of Wales. He led a long-running, but ultimately unsuccessful, revolt in the early 1400s against English domination. By 1404 he had gained considerable power and held a Welsh parliament in Machynlleth having won battles across Wales and its borders. However, his army then suffered several defeats during the time of Prince Henry and this brought the revolt to an end; his disappearance in 1412 remains something of a mystery. For more detail read David Perrott's Glyndŵr's Way Trail Guide, also published by Kittiwake.*

3 Go right here for about 50 metres, then turn left on a track by cottages where there are fine views across Knighton to your right. *It is from this vantage point that you can really see Knighton as the gap town, hemmed in by Garth, Ffridd and Panpwnton hills.* The green track leads into woodland beneath Garth Hill. Pass through a small gate, and follow the path as it bends to the right, dips a little and then rises gently up through the wood, a serene spot where you might hear the woodpecker at work amid the tall trees. Ignore paths and gates to the right down the hillside; keep ahead to leave the wood by way of a field gate and then along a green lane bordered in by tall hedges. This gives out to the appropriately named Rookery Lane. Keep ahead up to the triangular junction.

4 Turn right here to leave Glyndŵr's Way along a road signposted to Llangynllo.

Ignore the turning on the right to Craig-y-don, but keep ahead through a field gate by a cattle grid onto open access land, known as Racecourse Common or sometimes White Anthony. *In the 1800s it was one of Knighton's two racecourses holding regular meetings through to 1882. It is now covered in rowan, hawthorn and crab apple trees in addition to gorse so attracts a wide range of birds.* Leave the road to walk along a green track which peels off to the right and continue ahead for about 700 metres near to the fence line until the far end where it cuts the corner and returns to the hedge line. Look for a finger post on the right. Go through a field gate here and walk ahead to a second gate in the next boundary. Once through, turn left to walk alongside a hedge and through another field gate. Finally, climb a stile to join a lane. The views across to Knucklas castle are simply superb.

5 Turn right to walk along the lane as it winds its way down for about a kilometre, dropping steeply into Knucklas. *At the junction before the viaduct, go right and you'll see an interpretation board beneath the arches on the left, which explains this wonderful engineering feat, 13 arches, a span 23 metres (75 feet) above the valley floor and 174 metres (190 yards) in length.* Continue ahead to reach a bridge spanning the Ffrwdwen Brook. Those continuing should keep left over the bridge.

Station Link

If you are heading for Knucklas railway station or bus stop then turn right before the bridge, passing a stall which offers local produce from the community allotments, and just beyond to pass by the Castle Inn. Continue ahead at the junction by the inn; there's a bus stop for buses to Knighton opposite the bus shelter. Turn next right into Glyndŵr for the railway station at the top of the street.

Refreshments and Accommodation
Knucklas: Castle Inn, accommodation available in village

Bus and Train
Buses from Kington and Knighton to Knucklas and Lloyney, service 41
Railway halt at Knucklas

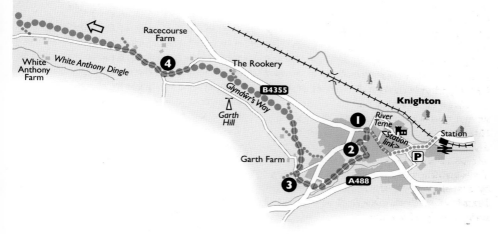

Dragon's Tooth sculpture, Knucklas Castle

5 KNUCKLAS STATION TO LLANBISTER ROAD STATION

18km (11 miles)

Cut off to Llangynllo Station

14km (8.3 miles)

This is by far the remotest section of the northern end of the trail, and the highest too, reaching 480 metres (1575 feet). It follows a ridge between Knucklas and Lloyney before climbing in earnest up to Wernygeufron Hill. The trail joins Glyndŵr's Way for a short distance then peels off across heather moorland to descend Cnwch Bank, crossing the infant Lugg and onward through meadows between Gravel and Llanbister Road.

Station Link

For those joining the trail at Knucklas see station link section above.

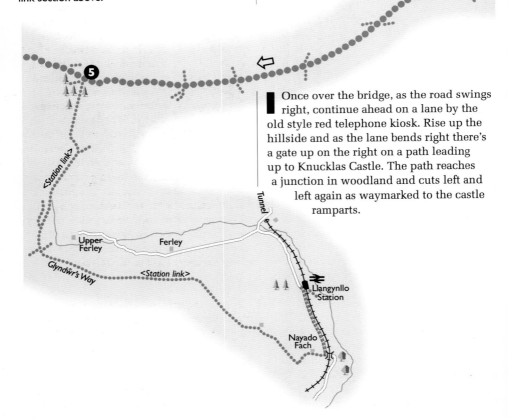

Once over the bridge, as the road swings right, continue ahead on a lane by the old style red telephone kiosk. Rise up the hillside and as the lane bends right there's a gate up on the right on a path leading up to Knucklas Castle. The path reaches a junction in woodland and cuts left and left again as waymarked to the castle ramparts.

*K*nucklas Castle *was originally built by the Mortimers in the early decades of the 13th century. There was by all accounts a stone keep with four round towers on top of this steep hill above the settlement. There is some evidence that there may have been additional outer walls; it is possible that they were destroyed by a Welsh army in 1262. Historians note however, that the castle fell into disrepair by the end of that century. Take a look at the sculpture which currently crowns the castle mounds; it is called Dragon's Tooth and is the work of*

but after approximately 100 metres turn left, through another field gate, and walk down a green track to a small hut on the right. Go right through a field gate and head up through a pasture to another gate. You are now heading along a ridge between the Teme and Heyop valleys. Continue uphill along a grassy track, through another gate and down a track to reach farm buildings. Turn right here to follow the tarmac lane for a kilometre as it winds down towards the village of Lloyney, passing a barn at a sharp corner and with a road coming in from the left part way down the hill.

Rolf Hook from Herefordshire. There's a superb 360 degree view from the sculpture.

The Castle and land below to the east is now owned by the Knucklas Castle Community Land Project. It has also planted a community orchard adjacent to allotments and is raising money to purchase the 21 acres of land. It is a testament to the villagers and especially to a small number of individuals who loaned the funds to make this project happen. Take a look at www.knucklascastle.org.uk.

3 Just ahead of the final bend before reaching the B4355 road (about 100 metres away), turn sharply left onto a holloway at a finger post. This leads up the edge of woodland, climbing steadily up to a field gate. Continue ahead, climbing again, through a second gate to really start climbing following the fence line on the left. Pass a pocket of trees and gorse. The path climbs steeply again, by a gatepost in a remnant hedge, and then eases up to the ridge. Continue ahead to pass a solitary tree which stands resolute on Goytre Hill; *there are superb views from this spot back along the ridge to Knucklas Castle from here.*

2 The path is waymarked through the castle grounds to the top of the ramparts so that you can admire the view and sculpture. You descend slightly right and then curve left past the scant remains of stonework to gently zig zag down the slope to a field gate on the western edge. Once through, proceed on a path ahead,

4 Proceed through a field gate onto Wernygeufron, to commence a walk along the common for nearly 4.8 km (3 miles) along a green track keeping the fence on your left. *This offers views across the Heyop Valley towards Radnor Forest to the east and rolling moorland to Beacon Hill to the west.* You climb slowly to a high point and then descend to a crossroads by a forestry plantation to join Glyndŵr's Way. *Lewis Davies in his book, Radnorshire, first published in 1912 (still going strong!), referred to this part as the 'land of mountain tracks' and a hundred years on who could say different. There are green tracks leading off in all directions.* If you wish to walk down to Llangynllo railway station or Llangynllo village for the Greyhound pub and accommodation see the Station Link.

Station Link

The most attractive way to walk to Llangynllo station is on Glyndŵr's Way, approximately 5 km (3 miles). Turn second left (not immediately left) at the junction, through a field gate to follow Glyndŵr's Way on tracks and paths to a lane, just before it cuts under the Heart of Wales railway. It is necessary to follow the Glyndŵr's Way waymarks thus far. Once on the tarmac lane, however, turn left to walk for about 600 metres to a small group of houses. Access is between the houses, through a double gate, to the platform; it is not immediately obvious. For those wishing to stay overnight in Llangynllo continue on Glyndŵr's Way for just under 2 km (about a mile).

5 Those wishing to continue along the Heart of Wales Line Trail will be able to reach Llanbister Road railway station in about 7 km (just over 4 miles) from the junction by the forestry plantation with Glyndŵr's Way. The main trail route follows it ahead across the common keeping the coniferous forestry plantation to your left. *The common belongs to the Crown Estate; there's more information provided at the interpretation board highlighting in particular the rich variety of wildlife to be found on this extensive upland.* After a while the track eases slightly right away from the fence and a woodland area known as Beacon Lodge to the left, climbing gently for a while. It then

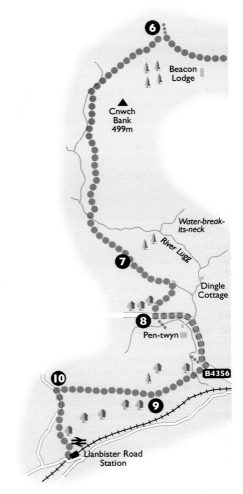

descends to two waymark posts; look for a bridleway branching off to the left.

6 Go slightly left along the bridleway, which is best described as an indistinct path across heather moorland. Proceed for about 2 km (just over a mile) following the waymark posts across the moorland, principally heather and bilberry or crowberry, as you head south and then south east to skirt a tributary of the Lugg surrounded by peaty wet ground. Drop down bracken slopes to cross the infant Lugg, *the river's name being a corruption of the Welsh word Llugwy meaning clear water. It certainly is at this point and the river is a Site of Special Scientific Interest throughout its course. It is little more than a trickle in summer, but you'll need to be more careful after heavy rain during winter months.* Part of the moor is managed by the Radnorshire Wildlife Trust and you might well see stonechats and meadow pipits, possibly curlew, red grouse, short eared owls, peregrine falcons or hen harrier on a winter's day.

7 Climb up an old track which curves slightly left to a small gate in a fence beneath an ash tree. Once through, continue ahead along a line of trees at first then a grubbed hedge to a field gate. Go through and in the next large field keep ahead with the hedge on your right. Midway down the field the path curves slightly left aiming for the bottom left hand corner. Proceed through another field gate. The trail continues ahead down a sunken track, rich in rush, but before reaching the hedge at the bottom climb out to go right along it to gate. Go through here and follow the clearer track down to another gate. Just after, with the ruin of Fronfelen to the right, cut left to walk along a wet sunken green lane to a field gate. This leads to the B4356 road.

8 Cross the road and go left to walk down it to Gravel chapel, seen on the left. Just before, go right through a field gate into a pasture and keep ahead. In the top left corner, go across a concrete footbridge into a wet meadow. Now head slightly left to avoid the really squidgy bit. Then continue ahead with a hedge to the left to a small gate. Go through it, turn right and proceed through a field gate. Once through, keep left by hawthorn trees to walk up to and through a field gate. Walk by Troedrhiwfedwen farmhouse, to pass through another field gate ahead.

9 Now proceed up the hill; the path heads towards the trees at first then curves right to climb up the hillside and through a field gate. Head very slightly right across a meadow to another field gate, and ahead again, this time through a traditional wild flower meadow to the next gate. *This is a rarity given that we have lost 97% of our wildflower meadows in the last 70 years, an astonishing fact reported by Hugh Warwick in his thought provoking work Linescapes.* Proceed in a similar direction in the next field to a gate which exits onto a lane.

10 Go left and the lane soon bends right where you go left through a second field gate. Head diagonally across the field; a communications tower below is a good marker. Pass through the field gate located between two woodlands and drop down the bank to a gate in the hedge on the right. Once through, head slightly left to walk over another concrete bridge and then slightly right to a kissing gate leading to Llanbister Road Station.

Refreshments and Accommodation
Llangynllo: link via Glyndŵr's Way to the Greyhound pub and accommodation

Bus and Train
Railway halts at Llangynllo and Llanbister Road

6 LLANBISTER ROAD STATION TO PENYBONT VILLAGE

14 km (8.3 miles)

with link to Penybont station

3 km (1.9 miles)

Climbing at first through rounded hills formed during the Devensian Ice Age, at least 18,000 years ago, the walk joins a byway through the foothills of the Radnor Forest to Llanfihangel Rhydithon, where there is a station link to the award winning railway station at Dolau. The trail then follows a winding lane which runs beneath Coed-swydd hill to pass by the historic Pales meeting house, before crossing Penybont Common into the village.

From the platform of Llanbister Road Railway Station walk up steps to the road. Go left over the railway bridge and then right at the junction signposted to Dolau. Walk along the road and look for the first field gate on the left. Go through here and climb up the hillside by the hedge on the right. Proceed through a second gate and continue with a hedge now on the left. Just beyond the top left corner pass through another gate and walk ahead to drop down to yet another field gate at the next boundary at the bottom of the field. Once through climb steeply up the bank heading slightly right. Continue in a similar direction, aiming for the buildings at Rhos farm. Descend through two small gates in fences and onto a tarmac lane.

2 Staying on the lane, go left to pass Rhos Farm and follow it up the hillside to reach a junction. Keep ahead on a track which passes through a field gate and descends into the valley. On reaching a stream, go through a field gate, turn left and then right to rise up the next pasture to another field gate beneath a line of veteran ash trees. Now climb more steeply to the summit. Take a look back at the panoramic

view before you reach the crest. *From here you can see the brooding mass of Radnor Forest ahead, an extensive hunting forest in medieval times. You will also see St Michael's Hall and pool to the left.*

3 Tempting though it is, do not follow the track down the hillside. Your way is roughly half right from the waymark post, below the brow of the hill walking through a long pasture. The path is indistinct but as you progress along the pasture you will see a patch of gorse over to your right near the top of the hill. From below that, make your way down to the field gate. Go through it and drop down to the pool below; it sometimes dries out in high summer. Continue ahead, beyond these old fish

pools, to climb up the hillside alongside a fence to your left, passing sheep pens at the top. You now join a clearer track which descends to a gate leading onto a lane.

4 Go left and walk along this quiet back lane as it winds down to a main road. Cross with care and follow the byway on the right, which climbs gently towards a pocket of woodland. *You pass by two old railway fruit vans, most probably dating from the early 1950s and sturdy enough now despite not having bogies or wheels.* Soon after you reach a field gate on the track ahead. About 150 metres beyond keep a look out for a fork in the track; keep left here on the lesser track which bends slightly left to a junction. Continue ahead, ignoring a track merging from the right to rise up through a gate; the track soon bends left to another junction. Take the right fork to dip down and follow the track as it curves right to a gate. Continue ahead to another gate, then along a wet section (in winter) beneath a coniferous wood. Descend to yet another gate where you'll see Old Hall to the right.

5 Keep ahead at the junction by a barn on the right with a pool and the Maes Brook on the left. Proceed through a gateway and field gate. Now climb up a tree lined sunken track and go through another gate at the top as it bends to the right. Walk ahead to a junction, where you keep left, ignoring a cattle grid and gate ahead. Continue to climb on the track, through a gate and onward to a cattle grid. Walk

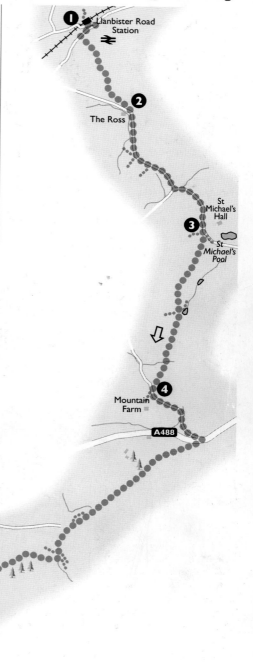

through two more gates by a barn and then drop down to a cattle grid after a junction for Pen Rochell farm. Keep ahead over the grid and on the track ahead until you reach a lane, where there's a station link to or from Dolau Station.

Station Link

For those wishing to finish their walk at Dolau station, there's a link of just over a 2 km, (1.2 miles). Go right down the lane, to the main A488 road where you can call in to see Llanfihangel Rhydithon church on the right. Otherwise, cross the road and go left for a few steps to a sign for the village and a finger post. Turn right through a field gate, ahead alongside a small pasture and through another two gates, across a drive, and over a stile. Keep slightly right across a large field to cross a stile in the next boundary and proceed in a similar direction to a stile leading into a cul de sac. Walk through to the lane then turn right and follow it to Dolau railway station, lovingly cared for by the Dolau Station Action Group for over two decades or more. The passenger shelter is packed with local information and historical references of interest.

6 Cross over and continue on a track between tall hedges until you meet another track coming in from the left. Keep right and drop down to a lane where there's a panoramic view ahead. Go left along this very quiet road which descends through a valley and then bends right through Kilmanoyadd farm. Continue to climb up to a T junction where you go right. Just after passing Rhonllwyn farm, keep right at the junction and rise up to pass the historic *Pales Quaker meeting house dating from 1716*. The road runs by an old quarry, through two field gates and cattle grid, to reach Penybont common and as it bends right, keep ahead by an old gateway post onto the common; there's no clearly defined path across it.

7 Proceed slightly right over a stream and head in a similar direction across the common, covered in part with rush and gorse. Head for a finger post on the common initially and then a second one at the side of the A488 to the right of an old poplar tree. On reaching the main A488 road, go left to walk on the green shoulder into Penybont, passing through a gate by a cattle grid, just before the Severn Arms Hotel in the centre of the village. Beware of traffic!

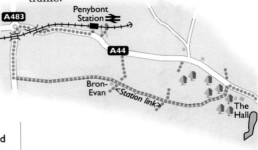

Station Link

The main A44 road to Penybont railway station suffers from fast traffic and is potentially dangerous. There are two alternatives. The station link is just over 3.5 km (2 miles). With your back to the entrance to the Severn Arms Hotel go left to walk along the pavement by the Thomas Shop. Cross over and continue ahead over the bridge and out of the village until you reach a road junction. Cross back over to walk up the lane which rises to a gentle ridge. Then walk down to pass a lane on the left and within a few metres another on the right. Follow the latter down the hill to the main A44 road. Go right on a narrow footpath which soon gives out, so you have to cross again to follow it up by old railway cottages to the turning on the left for Penybont station. The other alternative is to use the bus to reach Llandrindod Wells (or Penybont) railway station and take the train from there. The 461-462 Sargeants bus passes by the station entrance and terminates at Llandrindod Wells Railway Station (Mons-Sats only)

Refreshments and Accommodation

Penybont: Thomas Shop café, Severn Arms Hotel and accommodation
Cross Gates: one kilometre from Penybont station, accommodation and café

Bus and Train

Buses from Hereford to Llandrindod Wells serving Penybont, service 461-462
Railway halts at Dolau (station link), and Pen-y-bont (station link)

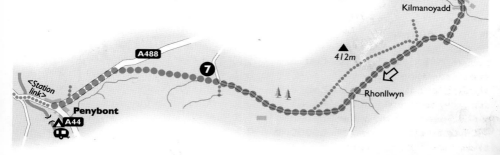

Pen-rhiw-garn

Kilmanoyadd

A488

412m

Rhonllwyn

Penybont

A44

Above Llanbister Road Station

7 PENYBONT VILLAGE TO LLANDRINDOD WELLS STATION

8 km (5 miles)

The trail leaves the village, passing near to Penybont Hall and by pools which are silted up and rich in vegetation. It then leads through pastures and a down a lane to the Ithon valley, with Cefnllys castle to the left and St Michael's church below. What a spectacular setting. Cross the Shaky Bridge to climb out of the valley and onto Bongam Bank and into Llandrindod Wells by way of the Lake.

For those arriving by train at Penybont read the station link note in the previous section. At Penybont road junction cross the road by the Severn Arms Hotel and turn left to walk along the front of the inn, but then cut right before the garage. A track leads down to the HQ of the local football club, bends right and then left to cross a footbridge over the flowing waters of the Ithon. Turn right to walk along the edge of the recreational ground and racecourse and then ease slightly left to proceed through a small gate adjoining double gates. Walk up the access road by houses to a lane. Turn right to walk to the corner.

In the very heart of the village the A488 meets the A44, both highways dating from the days of toll roads, which while expensive for users, brought more trade to a thriving village. Opposite stands the Severn Arms Hotel, built originally in the mid-18th century by the then owner of Penybont Hall, John Price, but the building seen today dates mainly from the mid-19th century. This old coaching inn would have been a stop for both the London to Aberystwyth stage coach as well as the mail coach from Knighton and Presteigne. Mr Price, who happened to be the founder of the Radnorshire Bank, spent

a considerable fortune on nearby Penybont Hall; the trail passes below it.

Penybont is also home to the amazing Thomas Shop, a trading concern, owned by the Thomas family. Four generations built a roaring trade in the 19th century focusing on groceries and draperies. This was a prosperous time for Penybont when people came from miles around to the hiring fairs and other seasonal events. The Thomas Shop is open to the public as a museum and galleries. It also has a café and is an absolute must to see.

2 Go left through a field gate to enter parkland and walk ahead to join a line of trees, bordering a pool to the right covered in reeds and grasses. At the top

Penybont Station

Greenfield Caely
<Station link>
A44

The Hall

Penybont

Bryn-Mawr

3

Bryn-Saesneg

Wainddu

Cwm Waunygroes

Neuadd Isaf

Afon Ieithon

Neuadd

4

Castle Bank 304m

Shaky Bridge

5

end, go through a small gate and along a tree lined path to a second small gate. Head slightly left across a pasture aiming for the second field gate; this leads into the next pasture, where you aim slightly right, climbing gently to a third field gate. There has been a diversion here at Brynmawr so older maps may well not show the new line of route. Cut left to pass between bushes down to another small gate and a winterbourne stream. Now head diagonally across the field to a field gate leading out to a track and a road.

3 Turn right along the road, around a bend and beyond an electricity pole look for a finger post on the right. Go through two pastures and small gates and then proceed ahead until you reach a third small gate in the hedge. Go

through it and head slightly right to exit at a field gate onto a lane. Go right and follow the lane through to the next junction. Keep ahead on a No Through Road. This rises up to Neuadd Isaf and then climbs again before a descent towards Neuadd. Drop down by a metal barn and a crossing of farm tracks where there's a small gate and finger post on the right leading into a field. Follow the track which bends slightly left to pass beneath Neuadd farm and through a

gateway. Dip to the right on a track through a field gate or over a stile. There are fine views as you drop down into the Ithon Valley.

*T*he magnificent defensive site of Cefnllys is to the left, high and mighty on the ridge; you can make out the ramparts above. In fact, the first castle, or as the Welsh word 'llys' suggests, may have been a fortified palace; it was built by Elystan Glodrydd in the 10th century, well before the arrival of the Normans. Subsequently, there were two Norman castles built here in the 13th century. Incidentally, some historians suggest that there might well have been an Iron Age hillfort preceding all of this too. The first Norman castle built by Roger Mortimer suffered dearly in 1262 as Llywelyn ap Gruffudd besieged the castle and routed Mortimer's Herefordshire men in the process. A second castle was built nearby to strengthen the command of the area,

35

referred to by John Davies in *The Making of Wales* as *Marchia Wallie*. This was the zone where Marcher lords held sway. Other parts of Wales were very much in the hands of the Welsh lords.

*H*ow many mediaeval warriors lived and perished here by the sword is not known. The castle was abandoned and so was the settlement which once stood near to St Michael's church below. This is despite having been granted a market charter in the 13th century. It might possibly have been a plague or continued ravages of war that resulted in a deserted village. The lonely church still stands. It dates from the 13th century, and retains a fine screen from the 15th century and bells from 1679; there are many other features dating from that period too so take a look when you are passing. In 1893 a rather zealous vicar had the roof removed so that parishioners would be forced to worship in nearby Llandrindod. 'No way!' was the reply and by 1895 the roof had to be restored at the princely sum of £1200.

4 Continue on a green track down to a field gate and once through keep ahead to St Michael's church. Pass through the kissing gate to the churchyard and, after you've taken a look at this much loved place of worship, go left through a second kissing gate. Head slightly left down to Shaky Bridge. It is no longer shaky so cross over without fear.

*B*ailey Einon Nature Reserve is managed by Radnorshire Wildlife Trust. It is primarily a broadleaf wood easing down the valley side to the Afon Ieithon, so wet ash, alder and oak pervade. Hazel is also widely found throughout the reserve and these are coppiced by volunteers to allow more light to reach the woodland floor, which encourages bluebells in the spring, as well as woodland favourites such as dog's mercury, red campion, yellow archangel and greater stitchwort. There are also some early purple orchids to be seen in spring. The reserve is also home to many lichens, mosses and liverworts as well as orange tip and ringlet butterflies found in woodland glades. It is worth a detour to enjoy the special feel of the place.

5 At the far end go through an ornate field gate, then a kissing gate on the right and immediately left through a small gate into a pasture. The path climbs in a crescent shape up to a kissing gate in the top left hand hedge. When you are through, go right to climb a little more on the road. At the junction keep left and follow the road until you see a path off to the left through a field gate; this is opposite Bailey Einon farm.

6 Walk up the field to pass through a small gate by a field gate into the next pasture. Continue ahead along the hedge line to another small gate at the summit. *There are exceptional views from here over to formidable Cefnllys and to Llandegley Rocks and Radnor Forest beyond.* Keep right to walk through a gateway (by an old broken stile) and then left through a small gate. Follow the green track which bends to the right along the shoulder of Bongam Bank. *There are some hidden earthworks in this area, thought to be the remains of a deserted medieval village, but barely discernible to the walker.* Do not follow the track all of the way up the bank; instead peel off slightly left, through scattered gorse and across a sheep pasture to aim for the pivotal point of the hedge. Cross the track and continue ahead in a similar direction towards a woodland belt, where you cross a path just before entering a dark tunnel beneath tall coniferous trees. The path joins another and gives out on the right at a stile into a pasture.

Bailey Einon Wood

7 Head very slightly left over to the nearest end of a gorse bank, where you'll see a narrow path dipping down the bank between gorse bushes to a small gate. Proceed through an oak woodland, keeping above a stream as the path leads down and eases slightly left to a gate in fencing by houses at Gorse Farm Estate. This exits onto to a road.

8 Cross over and follow the narrow path between gardens through to the same road. Go right and look for a corralled path on the left by a garden hedge. This bends right and then left to a kissing gate at a junction of paths. Head very slightly right up a field to cross a stile into rough ground, where you follow a compacted surface ahead. At the junction of paths go left and immediately right, so as to effectively continue straight ahead, rising up the hillside beneath a comforting canopy of woodland, part of the Lake Park at Llandrindod Wells. Go right at the crossroads to follow the path down to a road at the Lake. *The Lake was built principally for boating in the late 19th century and has been revitalised in recent years to encourage wildlife. Thousands of frogs and toads make a seasonal migration to the lake and this is quite some sight as is The Fabulous Water Beast said to be one of the largest public fountains in the UK.*

9 Cross the road and turn left to walk along the water's edge to a junction. Go right here to follow the path to pass by the old boathouse, now housing a café and restaurant. On reaching the road go left along Princess Avenue, left into Spa Road and across Temple Street (A483), ahead up Spa Road to pass by Temple Gardens and across the road to Middleton Street. Continue along what is Llandrindod's main shopping street to Station Crescent. Cut left here to the railway station and bus interchange.

Refreshments and Accommodation
Llandrindod Wells: shops, cafés, restaurants and pubs plus a range of accommodation

Bus and Train
Traws Cymru buses to Llandrindod Wells on the Cardiff to Newtown T4 service
Railway station at Llandrindod

8 LLANDRINDOD STATION to BUILTH WELLS (LLANFAIR YM MUALLT)

25 km (15.5 miles)

Cut off point at Newbridge on Wye (Pontnewydd ar Wy)

7 km (4.3 miles)

On leaving Rock Park, you'll be treading the ground where Roman soldiers trained, a gruelling affair no doubt. But you'll soon be beyond the jurisdiction of Llandrindod Wells, making good progress across the rolling green pastures to Newbridge-on-Wye. The trail then keeps company with the Wye Valley Walk identified with a marker, the leaping salmon. The shades of green make the semi natural woodlands exceptionally beautiful, offering a display of ferns, lichens and mosses as you make your way along the Wye towards Builth Wells.

Leave railway station from platform 2, on the opposite side to the ticket office, taking note of the London North Western Railway signal box which was at one time in service north of the station. You might also note the platform canopy which was taken from the Pump House Hotel, salubrious in its day; the hotel was demolished in the 1980s. Go right into High Street and then turn left to walk along it. As this rises towards a junction, keep right at the fork to walk through to a roundabout by a building known as the Gwalia (housing offices and Llandrindod Wells library). Cross Ithon Road, pass the entrance to the Gwalia, and proceed across Norton Terrace to the entrance to Rock Park.

Llandrindod Wells owes its existence principally to the properties of saline, iron and sulphurous waters associated with the healing of several medical conditions. Whilst the taking of the waters had been in existence since Roman times, it was the published work of Dr Linden in the 1750s which highlighted their value to a

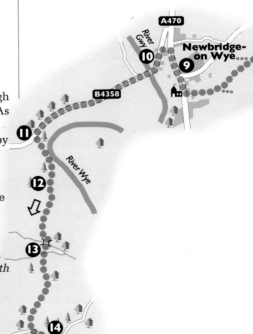

wider audience. The commercialisation of wells throughout the 1800s sparked a considerable growth in the town. Needless to say it was the coming of the railway in 1865 and a continued interest by the wealthy that brought a boom in hotel building, and the provision of parks and gardens throughout. It was described by one Victorian writer as 'the Montpelier of Radnorshire' and by another as the 'Queen of Welsh Watering Places'. Another newspaper commented that Llandrindod was 'responsible for more engagements than any other town of its size in Wales'. The air must be good.

*T*here is an excellent heritage trail which you can follow around town; it allows you to explore the rise and decline of spa life in Llandrindod through the ages. Middleton Street, for example, was once a street of boarding houses and some of the existing retail outlets retain cast iron and woodwork characteristic of the spa era. The trail passes along High Street, at one time the retail centre of the town, where there are fine balconies, wrought iron work and the renovation of beautiful Victorian buildings as part of a Townscape Heritage Initiative in the first decade of the 21st century. The nearby Gwalia was once a prestigious hotel with fine features to match; it has octagonal turrets topped out with ornate domes; such architectural designs were very fashionable in the Edwardian period.

2 Walk down the path to a road by the Rock Spa building, a former pump room which now houses a café run by the Spa Town Trust. *However, at the crossing of paths beforehand, cut left over the footbridge spanning the Arlais Brook to take the waters for here's a remarkable survivor, a chalybeate marble drinking fountain dating from 1879; you are welcome to top up your water bottle here!* At the road by the Rock Spa building, turn left then within a metre or so as to climb up steps on the left to a junction by a lamp post.

3 Go ahead to leave Rock Park along a path between a fence and hedge to exit on a road; *this is an area where Roman soldiers once trained for armed combat against the Silures, an indigenous tribe that fought with considerable ferocity against the might of the Roman Empire. The site of the Roman camp, Castell Collen, is near to the town.* Turn left to walk up Park Lane. This exits onto the Wellington Road

(A483). Turn right and walk along the pavement next to the highway (right hand side) until it gives out before a junction. Turn right here to walk over a road bridge above the railway. Almost immediately after the bridge turn left through a field gate.

4 Follow the track ahead through two field gates, passing through sheep pens so expect it to be trodden down and muddy in winter. Continue alongside a fence at first, but then peel off slightly left to go through a small gate. Once through, head slightly right towards the coniferous plantation. Proceed through a small gate; the path curves right, left at first, then ahead through the wood to a fence at Holly Barn. Go through a small gate, just to your right, onto the drive, turn left to walk along the boundary fence and left again through another gate back into the wood. Turn right to exit into a field by a small gate.

5 Keep ahead alongside the hedge; there are superb views across to the Cambrian Mountains (right) and Carneddau range (left) on this section. Cross a stile by a field gate and continue ahead with a hedge to the left. Go through a small gate and within 30 metres turn left through another gate and then right; you now walk alongside a hedge to your right and there's a farm beyond. Turn right on to the road and then left over a stile before a junction. Head very slightly right in the pasture. Exit through a small gate to a track and go left. This curves right and descends to a corner where you go over a stile into a field. Keep ahead and you'll see Red House farm to the right across the pasture. Climb a stile by a field gate and go left down to a wood and footbridge across a stream.

The Cambrian Mountains (Mynyddoedd Cambria) can be seen ahead, uplands described by English Victorian writers as the 'Green Desert of Wales', referring to the very remote upland plateau of rough moorland vegetation, bogs, and forests dissected by narrow river valleys. Yes it still is wild in many respects, but in no way a desert. These uplands are rich in biodiversity, with some 17% of land being designated as Sites of Special Scientific Interest. The Cambrian Mountains Society continues to campaign for designation as an Area of Outstanding Natural Beauty, so as to afford protection from unwanted development. The Cambrian Mountains provided the last refuge of the Red Kite in the mid-20th century and following a number of bold projects the Kite is well established again. The challenge is now how to avoid the collapse of other bird populations such as the golden plover, dunlin, and curlew.

6 Once across the footbridge, head slightly right through tussocks of grass and over a gully; this is likely to be welly wet in winter. Ease slightly right now, heading towards a boardwalk, and then cross a stile in the hedge. Turn right through a small pasture to climb to a second stile by a field gate. Walk up to cross a third stile beneath hazel bushes and continue ahead with a hedge to the right. *There are great views across to the Cambrian Mountains from here and, Disserth church soon comes into sight below in the Irfon Valley. This pretty little church is mainly from the 17th and 18th centuries with a pulpit dating from 1687 and box pews from the 18th century.* Make your way down to a field gate, pass through it and keep ahead to walk alongside the wood's edge to drop down to a stile onto a road opposite Disserth Caravan and Camping Park.

7 Go right over the road bridge spanning the Afon Ieithon and within 20 metres turn left through a small gate and ahead across a riverside meadow. Cross a footbridge into Berth-lwyd wood and keep left at first, but then bear right to climb steeply up steps and onwards along the edge of the wood, before climbing over a stile into a field. Go ahead with a hedge to the left to cross a stile, over a track and through a small gate into a pocket of woodland.

8 Cut right to skirt it, tip-toeing gingerly through wet ground to follow a hedge on your right as it curves around to a small gate. Continue ahead and you soon pass through another small gate in the next field boundary. Within a few metres turn right through another small gate and left across the field to a line of trees. Pass through a small gate and continue ahead down a bank, over a stream and across a field to rise up and through another gate. Now continue ahead up the next field to climb over a stile beneath a tall tree. Within a few metres (where the path forks) peel off left across this pasture. Continue through a small gate beneath a large oak tree in the next boundary. Proceed ahead, aiming for a field gate situated to the left of bungalows. Go through it and walk ahead along a green track, across Meadowlands road and onward between a school on the left and a sawmill to the right. You soon reach the main road; the 19th century church stands opposite. Turn right along the pavement to pass the ornate glass porch of the former Crown Temperance Hotel.

Newbridge-on-Wye (Pontnewydd-ar-Wy) was a place where drovers, whilst taking their stock to market, paused for refreshment at one of the many village hostelries. That is until the arrival of the Mid Wales railway between Three Cocks Junction and Moat Lane Junction in 1864, when livestock began to be moved by train.

9 Continue along the main road to pass by the New Inn on the right and ahead by the village shop and post office. Walk up to an outdoor shop after the Golden Lion pub. Go left here on a narrow road, signposted as the National Cycle Network Route 4. This leads to the B4358; turn left to follow this over the Afon Gwy and out of the village to join the Wye Valley Walk, a path which is highlighted with a distinctive waymark roundel featuring a leaping salmon.

The Afon Gwy is one of the longest rivers in the UK, some 215 km or 134 miles from source to estuary with the Severn below Chepstow. Artists and writers seeking the Picturesque landscape have been enchanted by the river since the 18th century, but not so many were tempted to visit the upper reaches. They missed out. It is certainly one of the loveliest watercourses in the UK, one that has not been subjected to extensive canalisation or industrial encroachment. Having said that, it suffers from pollution and habitat degradation which affects wildlife and has reduced fish stocks in recent decades, especially the spawning Atlantic Salmon for which the river is rightly known.

On this section of the walk there are otters and water voles, but you are more likely to see the brightly coloured kingfisher dashing down the river, dippers bobbing up and down on protruding rocks and mallard ducks, swans and Canada Geese which rear their young on or near the river.

10 The trail follows the B road ahead which is wide, but be wary of oncoming traffic. *You will see the parkland leading up to Llysdinam Hall, an early 19th century house often visited by Francis Kilvert, the most notable of rural Victorian diarists who was at one time curate of St Harmon parish near Rhayader (Rhaedr). The road rises steeply through forestry at*

Estyn Pitch and not before time, as you'll have had your fill of traffic. As it levels off look for a finger post on the left indicating that Builth Wells is 10 km (6 miles) away.

11 Cross with care to go through a small gate into Estyn wood. The path dips down through mixed woodland where you'll hear, but not see the rippling waters of the Afon Gwy. There are several boardwalks to ease access across wet sections, until you exit through a small gate into a field. This heralds a particularly lovely section of the Wye Valley Walk, at first through rich pastures and parkland and then along the banks of the Wye, shaded by mature oaks, ash and alder.

12 Head slightly left to climb up the bank; you will not catch sight of the next gate until you reach the brow. Proceed across the pasture to a small gate by a field gate and walk alongside a row of healthy hazel bushes to another field gate, then down to a gateway beyond a marshy area. Head slightly left across the field to a fingerpost before the edge of a wood. Bear right to descend the bank to the Hirnant, a babbling brook beneath trees. There's a guide rail to help here.

13 Go over the footbridge; continue ahead through spongier ground to a small gate and onward to a stile next to a fingerpost. Proceed through a pasture to pass through another small gate and head slightly left through a field towards the right hand end of a wood and through to a stile. Cross the stile and keep ahead to join a hedge on the right. Follow this to a field gate in the top right corner. Go through and now follow the hedge to the left to reach a fingerpost. Ease away from the hedge to walk down to a small gate in the bottom corner by a wood. Go through and walk along the fence to a kissing gate leading onto a road.

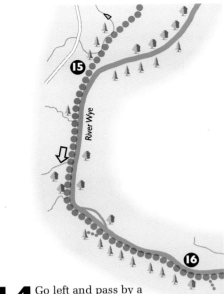

14 Go left and pass by a lodge and then right at the corner to walk through a small gate and wood to exit by way of another small gate. Aim slightly left across the field towards Porthllwyd farm. Enter the outer yard by a small gate next to a field gate and cut immediately right and then left alongside a barn to a second small gate. Pass through here and walk slightly right across the field to join a fence. Brynwern Hall stands in woodland to the right. Follow the fence to a small gate at the woodland edge. Once through, follow the woodland's edge to a footbridge across a stream and another small gate.

15 The path climbs to the right of a dwelling and across a path to the top of the wooded bank. Follow it ahead over worn tree roots and eventually you cross a footbridge to leave the wood. Proceed through four pastures and gates (and over one footbridge) to come to Goytre Wood. Go through a field gate and follow the main woodland track for about 100 metres *where the Wye Valley Walk peels* off left at a fingerpost and runs through wonderful woodland with mature sessile oaks, home to a staggering number of insects, and providing a canopy with other native trees overlooking the river. You'll see luxuriant growth of ferns and mosses here. Needless to say, you soon arrive at a wedge of coniferous trees where little else grows; cross a stile here and keep ahead over another stile by a field gate beneath Rhosferig Lodge.

16 The path joins a lane just beyond. Climb up the bank to a cattle grid at the corner where you

17 Pass beneath the railway bridge and then climb up, alongside ugly security fencing to a junction in Wern Wood. Keep ahead near to the river where you'll catch glimpses of the rapids at Penddol rocks described by the Reverend Warner in Walk through Wales (1797), as follows:

'The river appears at our feet, dashing and roaring through a bed of misshapen rocks, and forming in its struggles, numerous whirlpools, eddies and small cascades...beautiful meandering stream, the theme of poets and the fruitful subject of tourists...'

Walk through a kissing gate and proceed through four pastures and small gates and over one sleeper-bridge. The path turns right and makes its way to a small gate onto a road. Go left and left again over a bridge. Turn left for Builth Wells town centre following the tree lined promenade, known as Abrams Folly initially when planted by Mr Abrams, but look how grand it is now. It leads to the bus stops by the Wye Bridge near to the

peel off left through two gates into a large field. Dolyrerw farm is across the field to the right. At the end of the field, go through a gate and continue to walk along the riverside fence in another expansive pasture leading to a small gate. Continue through two more pastures and gates plus a footbridge, to enter Dolyrerw Wood and another stretch of mixed woodland on a path which is root riddled so neat footwork is required. Go through a kissing gate and stay near to the river (not the tarmac lane).

statue of a Welsh Black bull at The Groe. There are toilets here on the right in the car park and this is the principal bus stop for all buses to and from Builth.

Fabulous Water Beast, Llandrindod Wells

Station Link

Builth Wells to Builth Road railway station 3.5km (2 miles)

From the Welsh Black statue and by the main bus stand in The Groe, go ahead to the bridge over the River Wye. Turn left to follow the A483 road to a roundabout. Turn left to walk along the pavement passing by the Royal Welsh Show Ground. Cross the main road opposite the Royal Welsh Showground with care and proceed along it. At the end of the showground turn right into a road signposted as RWAS. This soon turns right into the ground, but you continue ahead up a lesser track and as it swings left, turn right onto a sunken lane to rise up through a gate and to a junction. Go right here to walk towards Lower Llanelwedd Wood. Choose the gate on the left to enter the wood and climb up, keeping ahead through two successive junctions. Ignore the next junction left and pass through a gate with a dwelling on the left.

At the T junction with Club Lane, go left to wander down this ancient thoroughfare, wet in places, but offering great views across Mid Wales. This eventually exits onto a lane at Cwmbach. Turn left to the old main road. The village of Cwmbach has been by-passed by a new stretch of highway and the old road is now very quiet – climb up to a bend. Cross over and

walk beneath the new bypass bridge. The path curves around to the left, then right to a gate and onto the road down to Builth Road Station. It is not immediately obvious but you need to access the station platform by way of a gateway to the right of the row of station houses. If you have time, take a look at the exhibition at the bus shelter by the old post office and Cambrian Arms *(at one time the low level station refreshment room for the Mid Wales Railway, opened in 1864 and closed to passenger traffic in 1962). This illustrates the development of the settlement in the late 19th century to accommodate passengers, freight and railway workers. The Cambrian Arms was closed at the time of publication.*

Refreshments and Accommodation

Newbridge: New Inn and post office and shop

Bus and Train

Traws Cymru buses to Builth Wells on the Cardiff to Newtown T4 service

Buses from Builth Wells to Llandrindod Wells some via Newbridge, service 44

Buses from Llandrindod to Llanidloes and Aberystwyth also serve Newbridge-on-Wye, service 47

Railway halts at Builth Road (station link to Builth Wells), Llangammarch and Llanwrtyd

9 BUILTH WELLS (THE GROE) TO LLANWRTYD STATION
22.5 km (14 miles)

Cut off at Llangammarch Station
16 km (10 miles)

The trail soon takes to higher ground rising over the shoulder of Moelfre, above the secluded Cneiddion valley. It then joins the Epynt Way to skirt Mynydd Epynt and if you enjoy panoramas there are some spectacular views across to the Cambrians as you drop down into the old spa town of Llangammarch Wells. The onward trek leads down lanes, and across the characteristic rhôs pasture of Mid Wales, thus it will be wet where the trail crosses the infant Cammdwr.

1 From the main bus stop (The Groe) by the statue of a Welsh Black bull, turn left to walk along the tree lined promenade by the River Wye, part of the Wye Valley Walk. The path cuts left to follow the Afon Irfon to a footbridge. Do not go over the bridge but continue alongside the river a short distance, where you leave the surfaced path to walk slightly right along a green track up to the A483 road. Cross over and proceed into Irfon Bridge Road.

*B**uilth Wells** (Llanfair ym Muallt) is a small market town with a spa heritage. It blossomed in the 1860s with the arrival of the railway, and whilst not as famous as Llandrindod Wells, it retained a reputation as a health resort for several decades. The Welsh derivation of the name means ox pasture or wild oxen in woodland. Following the departure of the Romans, the town and surrounding area became a small kingdom ruled over by Elysan Glodrydd. It eventually succumbed to the Normans when Marcher lord, Philip De Braose, built a substantial castle near to the Wye; this was rebuilt in the 1270s under the order of King Edward I to guard the river crossing point. The castle motte*

is still there although there's no stonework. In 1282 the last Prince of Wales, Llwelyn ap Gruffudd, was slain by the English near Cilmeri, marking a turning point in Welsh history for administrative counties were established under the aegis of the English sovereign and the Marcher lords gained even greater powers in the borders.

The bronze statue of a Welsh Black bull in the Groe, crafted by Gavin Fifield, weighs in at a solid 1.5 tonnes. It reflects the importance of cattle to the area in past times, although sheep farming dominates in most areas. Tourism has played its part too. Francis Kilvert commented, for example, that 'a beautiful enchantment hangs over Builth'. Many of the town's buildings date from the late 19th century, a boom time for tourism. The spas have now gone, but the Royal Welsh Showground still remains important for events and shows throughout the year.

2 The road rises to a corner and layby where you cut half right over a stile and footbridge to follow a charming path between gardens and the river. The path crosses a tributary stream and bends left upstream for a short narrow section, before

45

turning right to run between fences to Nant-yr-Arian, where you'll pass by a line of cottages. *The Welsh Nant-yr-Arian is roughly translated as a stream of money or silver. This refers to a time when plague had devastated the town and country folk were asked to leave produce at this point. In return the stricken townspeople would throw money into the stream as payment, hoping that the running waters would purify the coinage.* Walk up to a junction and go right to leave the town.

3 Within a few metres, go left to cross a stile by a field gate. Climb up the field alongside the wood leading down to a stream on your left, to cross a stile by a field gate into a green track. Continue ahead to cross a third stile and onward along the track, with a wooded slope where badgers and bats live; the track gives out at a gate into a field. Follow the hedge on the left up to another field gate. Go left through it and climb up with a hedge now on your right. Ignore the first gate, but turn right through the second one to follow a track which bends left, through a gate, passing between stables and a bungalow at Lower Hall Stables.

4 Go left onto the road to walk up by a community hall and a church where there are good views back over Builth. Just past the church, the road then bends left and at this corner you turn right to walk along a track; there's a

bungalow on the left. Keep ahead to walk through three field gates and with a barn to the right. Continue along a corralled track and then follow the fence on the left down to the woodland, through a pasture where horses are often kept. *There's a sense of serenity now, listening to bird song and looking at woodland flora which Mid Wales offers in abundance.* The track sweeps slightly left through the wood and leads down to another field gate. Go through and follow the hedge to your left down to another field gate. It now descends more steeply, over the Cneiddion brook, and through a final field gate.

5 Go left at the junction to climb up to a field gate leading into the yard of Brynbanedd Farm. Keep ahead on the track, through two more field gates to leave the farm behind. The clear track, bordered by common violets and celandine in spring, drops down left to a gully where it crosses a stream and rises up right through a field gate. The track continues to curve right, away from the stream and then bends to the left alongside a hedge. Go through another

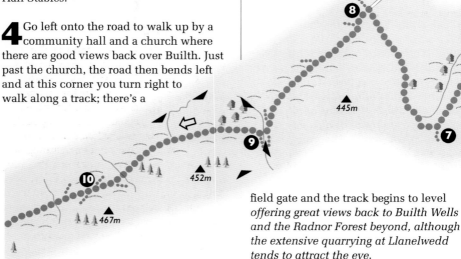

field gate and the track begins to level *offering great views back to Builth Wells and the Radnor Forest beyond, although the extensive quarrying at Llanelwedd tends to attract the eye.*

6 Proceed through a final gate to the open access hillside of Moelfre. Make sure to identify your route at this point! Once through the gate, leave the farm track at approximately 45 degrees (left) along a bridle path that is not well defined. Do not follow the main track which continues ahead and ignore the green track that goes straight up the hill parallel to the closed gate and fence to your left. Your route rises gently across the shoulder of Moelfre between windswept hawthorn and holly. It becomes more defined as you proceed. *In the spring you'll more than likely hear a cuckoo or two here seeking a mate in this valley. In due course, the female cuckoo stealthily lays an egg in each of the chosen host nests, usually that of the meadow pipits who frequent this patch of ffridd. There are excellent views of the valley below and across to the Cambrian Mountains.* Ignore another green path up the hillside on the left; keep ahead through a field gate into a pasture. Proceed ahead along a slope to another gate by a small outcrop, quarried in recent times.

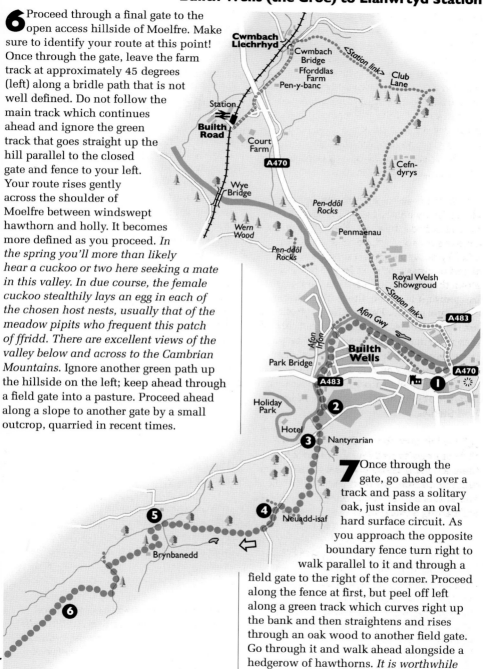

7 Once through the gate, go ahead over a track and pass a solitary oak, just inside an oval hard surface circuit. As you approach the opposite boundary fence turn right to walk parallel to it and through a field gate to the right of the corner. Proceed along the fence at first, but peel off left along a green track which curves right up the bank and then straightens and rises through an oak wood to another field gate. Go through it and walk ahead alongside a hedgerow of hawthorns. *It is worthwhile*

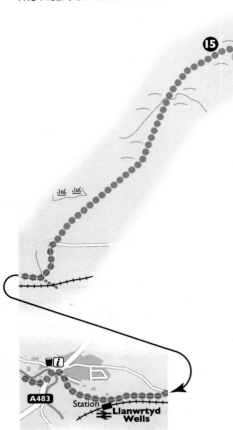

right you reach a junction. Keep ahead to rise up to a sunken track which curves slightly left through bracken and gorse to reach a junction, where you cut right to dip down to a stream and through a gate onto Ministry of Defence land, Post 20 to be precise, where there's a red flag. *Make sure you read the information provided, but be assured that it is possible to walk the Epynt Way even when training is in progress.*

*T**he trail** follows the Epynt Way for the next 3 km(1.9 miles). Epynt Way is an 80km (50 mile) permissive bridleway which skirts the Sennybridge Training Area on Mynydd Epynt, controlled by the Ministry of Defence. This western section of the Way offers exceptional views over the Irfon Valley to the Cambrian Mountains. The Epynt Way Association, which manages the trail, advises that you should not touch any military debris and that it is absolutely necessary to stay on the waymarked route through to the viewpoint located on the B4519*

pausing a while here, for there are superb views to be savoured right across Mid Wales. Proceed through a field gate then descend to another. Head down the field to a point to the left of the bottom right corner. Go through a small gate and ahead to another which leads onto a track.

8 Go left towards Pen-y-waun; the bridleway passes a stable and a drive leading off to the right. You, however, continue ahead through a field gate, turning immediately right on open access land. Proceed ahead near to the fence on the right where there are again good views across to the Cambrian Mountains. As the fence and another bridleway peels off

9 Go slightly right up a short sunken section beneath the finger post to a track known as Warren Road. Continue ahead along it. *It may well sound like you have entered a war zone, but do not be alarmed if you hear the distant noise of firing. There is an artillery range a few miles away and there might also be army exercises nearer. It does not seem to affect the skylarks and meadow pipits.* The Epynt Way path is very well waymarked; each post is topped with a yellow cap.

10 Beyond a junction of tracks come to Post 131 and here you leave the track and ease slightly right down the hillside. The path then curves left and climbs up, just to the right of the coniferous plantation, and left of the ravine, Cwm Graig Ddu, meaning Black Rock. It is to

12 Continue down this winding lane for 2 km or 1.2 miles right into Llangammarch Wells; it includes a right hand turn at a junction just before the village and merge onto the main road by the village post office. Keep ahead for the bridge over the Afon Irfon, where dippers and kingfishers can be seen. Head under the railway bridge and turn right to reach the railway station or, for those walking on, go left to continue to Llanwrtyd Wells.

your right, deeply incised and with the fast running waters of Nant-y-Cwm below, making its way to water green pastures. You are heading to the viewpoint on the road ahead – with a red flag usually flying a little further down the road. Keep ahead through wet ground and to waymark Post 138. Now proceed very slightly right, climbing more steeply up to the viewpoint so you might need a break! Go right by picnic tables and left up steps to the road.

11 You leave the Epynt Way here and head right, alongside the B4519 road until it reaches a cattle grid, where there are other road signs warning traffic about the military training in the area. At the right hand corner, leave the road to walk ahead down a green path, which passes by a solitary sentry hut and then twists slightly right and left across wet moorland. Follow the path down the ridge, through a field gate. There are exceptional views down to Llangammarch and beyond. Descend more steeply down to pass through two field gates just before a dwelling, Troed-Rhiw Isaf, at the foot of the hill. You'll pass a water wheel on the left, located on a site which was once a laundry. Keep ahead on the track to pass to the left of the house and then walk down a tree lined lane.

L *langammarch became popular as a spa town when barium springs were discovered here in the early 19th century. It was promoted as a diuretic for improving the health of the heart and kidneys. The village grew considerably in size, including the construction of several hotels, to meet the increase in visitors arriving by rail from 1867 onwards. The word 'wells' was added to the name at that time. A pump room was located in the grounds of the Lake Hotel and people enjoyed the waters here for several decades. Llangammarch was also a popular location for horse and pony fairs, but this ceased after the Ministry of Defence secured Mynydd Epynt (which means the mountain with horse paths) for training.*

The church of St Cadmarsh *sits opposite the railway station in Llangammarch, a building much restored in the early 20th century, but with many monuments dating from earlier centuries. Theophilus Evans was the vicar from 1738 to 1763, a time when he wrote his History of the Ancient Britons; A View of the Primitive Ages. His grandson, Theophilus*

Jones was also an author; he penned a work about the history of Breconshire. They are both buried here. There is also a commemorative stone to John Penry beside the Llangammarch church; John Penry was born at Cefn Brith near to Llangammarch in 1563. He campaigned for a Welsh bible and for there to be more preaching in Welsh. Unfortunately, his earnest endeavours enraged the then Bishop of Canterbury. Penry escaped to Scotland for a time, but when he returned to London he was imprisoned on spurious grounds and hung in 1593.

13 The route passes the Cammarch Hotel and follows the road out of the village, over a bridge, then rises up and over the hillside of Cefn Derwyn – *there's a welcome seat just over the brow.* At the first junction turn left, follow round a corner and onwards to the next crossroads. Take the narrow lane ahead, which is a no through road to leading to a small number of farms. This rises up to pass the entrance to Prysiau-fawr and then dips down where you take the gate ahead (leaving the lane) onto an unsurfaced track to Tyn y Rhôs. Follow this track through a gate and onwards to another gate leading into open access land.

There's a mixture of wet grassland and rush here, ideal ground for snipe and curlew, the latter much loved by Dylan Thomas and written about in some of his poems. Both birds have been in sharp decline since Thomas penned his greatest works so habitats such as this are essential for the birds to survive.

14 The line of the bridleway is not so clear on the ground here (this is, however, open access land). Head slightly left across the rough ground towards a pronounced gully, then walk on the near side of this to cross it before it gives out into a boggy area. Cross the infant Camddwr by a bridleway bridge and bear right to reach a gate to leave the open access land.

15 Through the gate there is no clear path across the pasture but walk towards a cluster of three trees ahead on slightly higher ground. Continue ahead beyond these and then aim very slightly left down to a gate by a small stream. Go through it and keep ahead, slightly right alongside a line of hawthorns and gorse, ahead over a gentle brow to a gate beyond which is a fenced-in track. You follow this attractive green tree lined bridleway through a series of gates all the way to the road. There's wetland to the right, the source of the Camddwr, which flows into the Afon Irfon. Turn right on to the road and follow it towards Llanwrtyd Wells. At the junction, keep left for Llanwrtyd railway station.

Refreshments and Accommodation
Builth Wells: shops, cafés, restaurants and pubs plus a range of accommodation
Llangammarch: post office and shop, Cammarch and Lakeside Hotels
Llanwrtyd Wells: café, restaurants, inns and accommodation plus a general store

Bus and Train
Traws Cymru buses to Builth Wells on the Cardiff to Newtown T4 service
Buses from Builth Wells to Llangammarch and Llanwrtyd Wells, service 48
Buses from Builth Wells to Llandrindod Wells some via Newbridge, service 44
Buses from Llandrindod to Llanidloes and Aberystwyth also serve Newbridge-on-Wye, service 47
Railway halts at Builth Road (station link to Builth Wells), Llangammarch and Llanwrtyd

10 LLANWRTYD STATION TO CYNGHORDY STATION

18 km (11 miles)

The trail climbs over the watershed between the Irfon and Brân rivers through Crychan Forest, an extensive area of forestry, and soon after zig-zags down to cross Nant Hirgwm on an old road to Clynsaer. It rises again through Gilfach farm on a bridleway, wet in places, but with wonderful views across to the Carmarthen Fans. The trail leads down to Llanerchindda before running beneath the magnificent Grade II listed viaduct at Cynghordy.

1 Turn left out of the railway station signposted to the town centre and walk to the main square where there are cafés/restaurants, a shop and hotel. Turn left again along the Llandovery Road (main A483 road) passing by the sculpture of the Red Kite. Once over the Afon Irfon, cross the road and walk ahead by St James's church, before turning right into Victoria Road. Follow this out of town. The road rises and bends left and right before levelling by three dwellings on the right.

Llanwrtyd Wells is the fourth spa town you'll encounter on the Heart of Wales line. The spa era here began with the discovery of the skin healing properties of water drawn from Ffynnon drewllyd (roughly translated as the stinking spring) by the Reverend Theophilus Evans in the early 1730s. Believe it or not, people were not put off by the smell and flocked here in their droves from south and west Wales. As with the other spa towns, it became immensely popular with the arrival of the railway in the 1860s. It is now a 'Walkers are Welcome' town.

Llanwrtyd claims to be the smallest town in Britain and yes, it is small, and there are only a few remaining shops. However, it is big when it comes to events- the World Alternative Games, World Bog Snorkelling, the Man vs Horse Marathon, the Real Ale Wobble and other unusual. pursuits (an understatement) which attract

thousands of visitors every year. The events are mainly down to one man, Gordon Green, who ran the Neuadd Arms for many years. Llanwrtyd also attracts those in search of wildlife and this is reflected in the amazing welded galvanised steel sculpture of a Red Kite in the Square, designed by Sandy O'Connor for the town. The Congregational chapel on Ffos Road has been renovated in recent years and is now the Llanwrtyd and District Heritage and Arts Centre where you can view contemporary art exhibitions and gain insights as to how important spa tourism was in its heyday.

2 Go left before a house on the left, as signposted, between a fence and the property to a small gate. Once through, head slightly right up the hillside to a field gate at the top. Go through and keep ahead in the same direction to join a track and then climb up to a junction, just before the brow of the hill. Turn right here to walk to the left of a covered reservoir *where there are superb views across the Irfon Valley to Mynydd Epynt.*

3 Proceed through a field gate and turn left. Follow the lane down, bearing left at a junction, to reach the A483 at Berthddu (meaning black hedge in Welsh). It is just under 2 km distance. *You'll see Sugar Loaf summit to your right.* Take care at the main road as you'll need to cross over and turn left for a few steps to the junction off right. Go right along the lane, across the railway track and then down to a stream, the Cledan, another tributary of the Irfon.

4 Follow the lane, over a cattle grid, as it climbs up to Bryn-hynog farm; go through a field gate and keep slightly right to head between farm buildings. Well before you reach the farmhouse, keep right along a track to descend slightly to a field gate. There are often caravans in the field to the left. Continue ahead to go through another field gate, and follow the track slightly left on a green track, to climb up the hillside in earnest now. However, be vigilant; look for a field gate about 150 metres on the right. Pass through it, and

then cut left to climb a steeper section, leading up to a gateway and a top pasture. Go through it and head slightly right towards a field gate and finger post near to the woodland, where another bridleway joins before entering the wood.

5 Go through the gate into Crychan Forest, managed by Natural Resources Wales. A track leads into the woodland and if in luck you'll see jays here amongst the moss covered trees. The trail crosses a wider forestry track and then climbs at first before descending and bending right. This joins another track, keeping right on this old drovers' way through the forest. Ignore junctions to the left and right to continue ahead on a well rutted route which is worn down to bare rock in places. *This can be challenging in places as not only have the 4x4 vehicles brought about a degradation of the main track, but also adjacent areas have been churned up making it difficult in winter.* It finally descends gently for a couple of kilometres to a road.

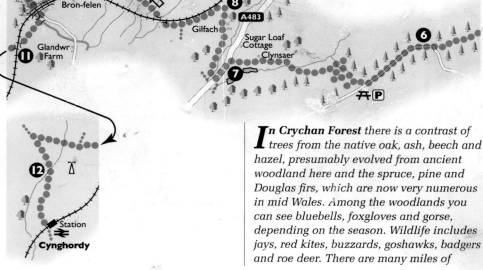

In Crychan Forest there is a contrast of trees from the native oak, ash, beech and hazel, presumably evolved from ancient woodland here and the spruce, pine and Douglas firs, which are now very numerous in mid Wales. Among the woodlands you can see bluebells, foxgloves and gorse, depending on the season. Wildlife includes jays, red kites, buzzards, goshawks, badgers and roe deer. There are many miles of

way-marked routes on forest roads, criss-
crossed with old tracks and drovers' roads.
The trail, for example, passes a mid-way
point known as Cefn Llwydlo meaning
Ludlow Ridge, which is a reference to one
of the English destinations visited by these
hardy Welsh drovers.

6 Keep right on the road,
passing the entrance to
the Esgair Fwyog car park.
Continue ahead along the
road until you reach a finger
post. Cut right here into the
wood, through wet ground
at first then follow the
bridleway which winds
its way down the hillside
to reach a junction near the
bottom. Go across the forestry
track and walk down to a point
near a fence, where you go left
along a narrower overgrown
section of bridleway, crossing
streamlets and wet ground
before coming alongside
a fence to a small gate.
Go through it and walk
alongside a sunken lane
down to Nant Hirgwm.
Cross over a bridge and
follow the green track
half left up to a field gate;
go through it and left along
the lane beneath Clynsaer
farm and by other
dwellings to the
main road.

7 Cross the road with care,
turn left for 20 metres and
then right through a small gate into
a field. Make your way left along the
field's edge to go through a field gate
to join a track. There's been a recent
diversion here so if you have an
old map it will not be shown at this
point. Once over the stream, turn right
along the track to follow it up to Gilfach
farm. Proceed through a field gate, keep
to the left of the farmhouse and yard to go
through a second gate.

8 The track rises up to the railway line,
but just beforehand turn left to follow
the field hedge on the right alongside
the railway. Walk through the first field,
through a field gate and proceed through
a second field keeping the same direction.
*There are super views ahead to the slopes
of Dyffryn Tywi.* Continue ahead to a field
gate, which you go through to cross the
railway with care, and now you are in the
land of really wet rough pasture. Follow
the line of oaks ahead to another gate, cross
a stream and then follow the hedge line
through a second wet pasture to the next
field gate to join a clearer and much drier
farm track.

9 Follow this as it bends right and then
up to a junction, where you keep left
through a field gate. The track bends right
and then left over a small brow where
you keep slightly right (not slightly left
along the track), through rush cover with
a fence to the right. Pass through a field
gate and go ahead to rise beneath an oak

Llwyneuadd

Ty'n-y-maes

Berthddu

A483

Henbant

Penmaenllwyd

Llanwrtyd
Wells

Station

A483

Bryn-hynog

Crychan
Forest

Cefn-Llwydlo

Cynghordy Viaduct

tree. *There are good views back over to the Carmarthen Fans from here.* The path now runs alongside the tree line and fence to your left. Go through another gate and very wet ground, as the bridleway descends to a gate. Pass through and walk a drier tree lined track, which drops down to a gate leading onto a lane below Llanerchindda.

Cynghordy Viaduct, one of the most challenging structures engineered on the line, is a wonderful sight. In addition, the Sugar Loaf tunnel at the head of the Gwyddon valley was equally difficult to engineer. The efforts of the railway pioneers and that of the hundreds of navvies working on the line were rewarded in 1868 when the line was complete. The viaduct has eighteen arches, built in sandstone and lined with brick and is 259 metres long on a gentle curve, rising to a height of 31 metres above the valley of the Afon Brân.

10 On reaching the road, turn left to follow it down to the foot of the viaduct, stepping beneath the magnificent arches of this superb feat of engineering. Go next right over a footbridge over the Afon Brân, through a narrow gate, and ahead on a lovely old tree lined trackway to cross the railway; take care here. *This might well have been an old drove road as Cynghordy was known to be a resting place for drovers.*

11 The track climbs beneath trees and then then bends slightly right alongside a fence and through another field gate. Proceed to a waymark post and the track bends right to a stream and narrow gate. After crossing the stream continue 300 metres ahead across rough rushes and tussocks to the right hand corner of the first field, then aim for the left hand corner of the second field. At this point bear left, then walk alongside the hedge/fence (south easterly direction) for 250 metres until reaching a small gate on the right. Proceed through it and turn sharp left alongside a fence to a little bridge.

12 Go over the bridge and cut left through a field gate and turn immediately right up to a second field gate. Once through, keep ahead. You need to head slightly left along the hillside through an old field boundary. Now aim to the right of a barn where you pass through a field gate. Continue ahead onto a drive and through a small gate by the cattle grid. The drive curves down to a stile where you cross the railway again with care. At the junction cut left for Cynghordy railway station.

Refreshments and Accommodation
Cynghordy: range of accommodation
Bus and Train
Railway halt at Cynghordy

11 CYNGHORDY STATION TO LLANDOVERY STATION

11 km (6.8 miles)

You start by walking along lanes beneath beautiful green canopies in the scattered settlement of Cynghordy, the English translation of the place name means Meeting House. Jays and Greater Spotted woodpeckers love to frequent these woodlands; you might catch sight of one. The trail then makes a way through pastoral farming country, before dipping to Dolauhirion Wood and through tranquil water meadows alongside the Afon Tywi.

1 Leave the station entrance and walk ahead down a lane lined with willow and thorn to a junction at Cwmcuttan. Go right at the first junction and right again at the second to pass through a tunnel beneath the railway. Follow the lane up the hillside, with a lovely array of roadside flowers which begin in the spring with celandine, wood anemone and wood spurge, giving way in summer to wild strawberry, campion and common dog violet. Follow the lane until it bends sharp right. You go left here, through a field gate, then on a track to a second gate and footbridge over Nant Bargoed.

2 The track rises up to pass an old farm, and soon becomes a surfaced lane passing a dwelling, before reaching a junction. Keep ahead at the junction to rise up to a summit, *where there are excellent views across to the Carmarthen Fans.* Follow the winding lane down to a point where there's a drive on the left to Cefnllan. On the right is a small gate and footbridge. This is your way into a large field where you head very slightly left to skirt a protruding field corner, and through wet ground, to cross a footbridge over a stream.

3 Cross a stile into the next field and head very slightly left again to go through a field gate. Proceed in a similar direction across another wet rush pasture to cross a stile, just beyond a small stream, about 20

metres to the right of a corner. Once over, go straight ahead to the bottom of the slope (clear of the very wet ground) and then left parallel to the stream. Cross a stile just to the right of the stream, often surrounded by mud, and continue ahead with a hedge to the right, although watch out for overhanging branches. The old track curves right up to Rhandirberthog Farm.

4 Go left on a track, before the farmhouse, which soon cuts right through Pantglas farm and continues to climb, with sumptuous views across to the Brecon Beacons, until you reach a junction. Turn left here and walk down the lane for just over a kilometre to reach Maes-y-gwandde farm on the right. Go right after the buildings and farmhouse down a concrete road, passing through two field gates; it then becomes a track which soon bends left to descend into the valley. The track then curves right, passes through a field gate and climbs up to a hairpin bend, cutting left to rise to Cefnrickett farm. Go through another field gate as the track bends right towards the farmyard and house.

5 Do not go up to the house. Your way is left, climbing over a stile by a field gate. Now turn right to walk along a green track with a hedge on your right. Go through a gateway and head very slightly left down the hillside. *There are excellent views across to the Brecon Beacons from here.*

Cross a stile by a field gate in the field boundary and continue ahead to the next hedge with woodland to your right. Climb a stile and keep ahead again to enter the wood along an old track, which curves slightly right to a field gate. Go through and then look for a stile on the left. Cross this and drop down the field to go through two small gates, one either side of a track.

6 On reaching the road, cross with care and turn left to the junction, then right towards the historic Dolauhirion Bridge, *designed by the Reverend William Edwards of Pontypridd and built by his son Thomas in 1773. The Field Magazine proclaimed it to be the prettiest bridge in Britain in 1961.* Before the bridge, cut left over a stile. Pass through two kissing gates, then along a corralled section between gorse bushes. Follow the field's edge

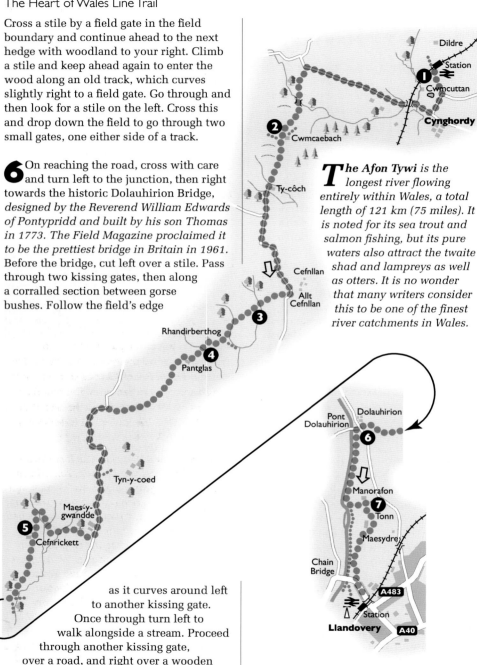

The Afon Tywi is the longest river flowing entirely within Wales, a total length of 121 km (75 miles). It is noted for its sea trout and salmon fishing, but its pure waters also attract the twaite shad and lampreys as well as otters. It is no wonder that many writers consider this to be one of the finest river catchments in Wales.

as it curves around left to another kissing gate. Once through turn left to walk alongside a stream. Proceed through another kissing gate, over a road, and right over a wooden footbridge and gate into a field.

7 Follow the hedge on the right around buildings at Tonn to cross a road guarded by two kissing gates. Follow the hedge to the right and pass through another kissing gate into the next pasture. Now head slightly right to go through a kissing gate before a shed with a corrugated iron roof. Go left along a green track, over a stile by a gate and head very slightly left alongside a hedge and through a kissing gate. Continue along a green track to exit through another kissing gate onto a main road to the left of a road bridge. This was once a fording point known by drovers to be extremely dangerous, many lost their lives here in times of flood. Turn left for the short roadside stretch to Llandovery railway station.

Refreshments and Accommodation
Llandovery: café, shops, restaurants, inns and accommodation including the Llandovery Railway Station café and gallery-not to be missed.

Bus and Train
Buses from Carmarthen to Llandovery, service 280/281
Buses from Lampeter to Llandovery service, 288/289
Railway station at Builth Road (station link to Builth Wells), Llangammarch and Llanwrtyd

12 LLANDOVERY STATION TO LLANGADOG STATION
19 km (11.8 miles)

George Borrow described Llandovery (Llanymddyfri in Welsh) as the pleasantest of towns he'd visited, and from here the trail rises through the foothills above the Tywi, and along a ridge clothed in deciduous woodland. It passes near the Welsh home of Prince Charles to the ancient settlement of Myddfai, home to a long line of physicians through the centuries. The trail rises again through rolling rich Carmarthenshire farmland, where old farms have stood the test of time, alongside ancient hedgerows and down lanes bordered by a rich diversity of roadside flowers, to Llangadog, a large village which offers refreshment and a bed for the night.

I Leave the station entrance and turn right to walk along the main road into Llandovery town centre. Look for the turning on the right by Llandovery tourist information centre and into a car park/bus stop to a point beneath the grassy mounds of Llandovery Castle. Just before the castle ruins, go left on a track beneath a statue, through a gateway to join a path along the riverside. Climb up steps and turn right to walk over the Waterloo Bridge.

L landovery (Llanymddyfri) was at one time an important resting place for drovers making their way through to the markets of England. They would often herd 300-400 Welsh Black cattle on route to Smithfield in London, sometimes augmented by geese, ducks and even corgis. One drover who grew rich on this gruelling existence was David Jones, who established the Black Ox bank in the town in 1799. Llandovery now seeks to develop tourism as well as agriculture and is a 'Walkers are Welcome' town. Like many other Welsh towns, it suffered Norman domination from early medieval times. Llandovery castle is clear evidence of this. Situated by what is now the eastern end of the town car park, the 12th century castle has seen developments come and go. It was built by the influential Norman lord, Richard

Fitz Pons, who fought alongside William the Conqueror. He was duly rewarded as a Marcher lord and given considerable freedom. However, the fortification spent most of its existence in the hands of Welsh commanders, a testimony to the resilience of people in these parts.

Llandovery has had many famous residents, including William Williams, originally from Pantycelyn, who wrote the famous hymn 'Guide me oh thou Great Jehovah', which is often sung at rugby matches. It was also home to Llywelyn ap Gruffydd Fychan, commemorated by the headless statue which stands beside the castle ruins. The statue was the work of Toby and Gideon Petersen in 2001, the result of a tireless campaign by a local man to have it commissioned. The statue is mounted on a 17 ton boulder and honours Llywelyn ap Gruffydd, who was hung, drawn and quartered by Henry IV's men as a warning to others not to support the Welsh leader, Owain Glyndŵr, following his unsuccessful attack on the township in 1401.

2 The road bends left and in about 100 metres turn right onto a concrete road, through a field gate and yard of Bronallt farm. Go through a small gate by a field gate and climb away from the farm, rising up through a kissing gate by a second field gate leading into a wood. Follow the path to a wider

track where you bear left and then right as the track curves right and continues to climb. At the fork, turn left and exit into a pasture by way of a kissing gate. Do not be tempted to follow the hedge line beyond the first corner; head slightly left up the hillside across a large field. There are great views across the Tywi valley, hewn out by a glacier to this flattened U shape, as you rise up towards the far corner (not the field gate seen on the horizon). Go through a kissing gate and continue to walk in the same direction across the next field, well to the right of the dwelling, Cefn-yr-allt-uchaf, which is situated on the left. Proceed through a kissing gate by a field gate, passing by pools and continue very slightly left to pass through a kissing gate in a fence. Continue up a drive through a kissing gate by a field gate.

3 In about 25 metres, the track bends left, but you go right to descend into the valley, heading very slightly left towards tall gorse bushes and a tree line. Go over a kissing gate by a field gate and walk

ahead along a tree lined track. You soon reach a junction, where you go left to rise up another tree lined track, over a stile by a gate and climb up the wooded hillside known as Allt Llwynywormwood referring to wormwood, an important herb used in medicine, but perhaps better known for its aromatic properties in the making of the rather more lethal absinthe. Cross a stile by a field gate and continue upwards to go through another gate; after 30metres or so you reach a crossing of tracks.

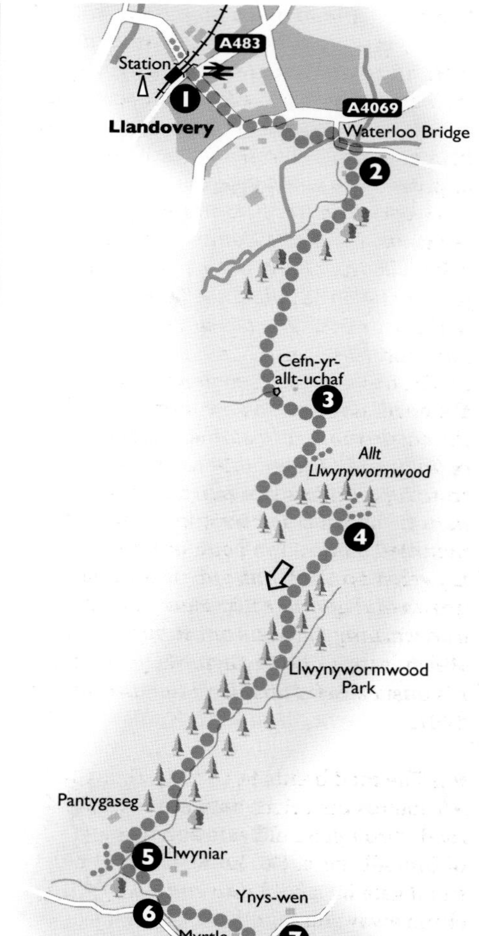

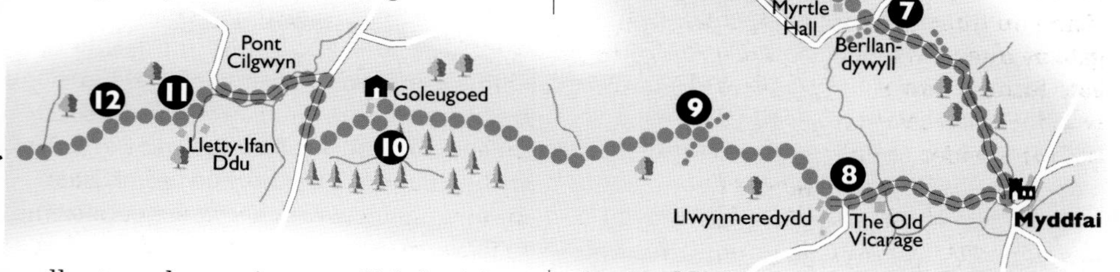

4 Go right through a field gate and wander along a track where young trees have been planted on either side. Pass by a dwelling on the right, as the track bends left and then right and descend through mixed woodland with views across to Llwynywermod Park, now in the ownership of the Royal Duchy. Ignore a track off to the left over a bridge spanning the Nant Mydan; your way is along the track which continues ahead, then bends right to go through a field gate.

5 Keep ahead along the side of the valley and you will see a farm, Pantygaseg, above to the right. The track curves right and at this point, look out for a small gate on the left. Cross it and drop down slightly left to cross a footbridge over Nant Mydan. Climb up the hillside towards the right of a bungalow seen above. Go through a small gate onto a track, turn right and follow this for about 20 metres before the track curves right.

6 You, however, need to keep ahead to climb up the valley side on a narrow path between tall trees of varying hues, which clearly like the rich habitat provided by this small ravine. Go through a small gate into a pasture and keep ahead near to the hedge on your left. Go through another

small gate and now aim very slightly right. Head to the left hand side of the cottage roof seen ahead at Myrtle Hill, and go through two kissing gates by the cottage onto a drive and ahead at the road (do not turn sharp left).

***M**yddfai has deep cultural roots, and is somewhere to linger awhile, to soak up the atmosphere of a distinctly Welsh village, made famous by the long line of physicians who lived here. The Red Book of Hergest (1382) includes cures offered by* *the Myddfai herbalists of the time, using plants found locally and pure water drawn from the physicians' well on Mynydd Myddfai. There's a stained glass window at the visitor centre which regales the tale of the Lady in the Lake (Llyn y Fan) and how her three gifted sons became the first physicians when she returned to the waters of the lake. Well, that's how legend would have it. The window was crafted by local people under the guidance of Lesley Griffith and Bernice Benton and unveiled by Prince Charles in 2017.*

In the centre of the village is Saint Michael's church, a listed building dating from the 13th century, although the circular churchyard suggests that there were earlier churches on the site. Despite restoration in the 19th century, the church retains many medieval features and contains memorials to two 18th century physicians. There are also two lovely chapels in the village. There's a welcoming café and shop at the community hall and the profits from this venture go to Myddfai Ty Talcen, a charity which helps to sustain this isolated rural community.

7 The lane ahead winds down between two woods, one being Coed Leter, managed by the Woodland Trust; you are able to walk around it if you wish. You soon arrive in the village of Myddfai, where you turn right by the church to pass Myddfai Community Hall and Visitor Centre. Continue along a narrow lane to pass by the entrance to the old vicarage and, at the next corner, go ahead through gates towards Llwynmeredydd Farm, the home of one of the physicians of Myddfai in a previous century.

8 Before reaching the house, turn right through double wooden gates and rise up a track through a scattering of trees, up to and through a field gate. Go immediately left through another field gate. Brace

yourself and climb up the bank, slightly right and then left, keeping to the right of a spinney of trees and heading for the top left corner of the field. Part way up, you will see an outcrop; that is where you are heading. Go through a gate in the corner and proceed ahead with a hedge to your left. There are marvellous views from this vantage point across to the Carmarthenshire Fans, especially Mynydd Myddfai and Mynydd Bach Trecastell. Go through a gate and ahead to join a cross roads of paths, where there is a cattle grid.

9 Cross the track and follow the hedge on the right up the bank for about 100 metres. At this point head half left across the sheep pasture (ignoring the stile in the opposite boundary). From this vantage point there are wonderful views across Carmarthenshire, small fields with winding hedges, pitted with pockets of woodland. Descend to the bottom left hand corner to cross a stile. Once over, keep ahead with a hedge to your left, but try to avoid a wet flush here. Go through a field gate ahead and descend again with the hedge left, through a second gate, and then ahead to pass through a third field gate to join a track by a wood. Go right through two gates by a barn above Goleugoed farm.

10 At the junction, keep left and as the track sweeps right, keep ahead across the pasture, aiming for the bottom left hand corner. Go through a field gate leading on to the road. Turn right and at the junction go left. Pass by Cilgwyn Lodge, with delightful gardens, and as you rise up the hillside go left at the finger post to proceed through a gate, marked Pistyll Gwyn, and climb up a drive.

11 As the track bends towards the dwellings, go right over a small footbridge and stile into a field, with Llety-ifan-ddu on your left, *a handsome* *late Georgian country house.* Keep ahead to climb alongside the boundary wall and fencing, to reach a stile by an old barred gate. Go over it and keep slightly right of the old quarry working, up a track into a field.

12 Climb steeply up the hillside, aiming very slightly right to go through a kissing gate by a field gate. Keep in a similar direction in the next pasture to another kissing gate, and follow the fence on the right through to a third kissing gate; keep ahead again. If you happen to have an older map, please note that there has been a diversion here in recent years so as to avoid Glasallt Fawr. Go through the second field gate on the right (approximately 50 metres after passing an old wooden chalet in the adjoining field to the right). Once through the gate, turn left to follow the fence around to the right, before descending slightly into a dip, and rising to a kissing gate in the far left hand corner of the field.

13 Pass through this kissing gate and drop down the hillside alongside a fence on the right. Halfway down, as the fence cuts right, keep right through an old tree line, and bear diagonally downhill towards a kissing gate in the bottom right hand corner of the pasture. Pass through the kissing gates and follow the path as it zig zags down to the access track to Glasallt Fawr, which is on your left.

14 Go straight across this access track and through a kissing gate, heading down to another small gate and track. Proceed through a kissing gate into a large field, keeping ahead along the hedgerow through another kissing gate. In about 100 metres, go through a gate on the left and then head slightly right across a field of wet rush, to exit at a kissing gate onto the A4069 road. Cross with care, especially looking for cars approaching at speed from the right.

15 Go left alongside the road and then right up a narrow lane which climbs at first, curves to the left and then levels with fine views over the Tywi Valley. Llangadog is about 3 kilometres (1.8 miles) away. The lane eventually descends, steeply in places to Llangadog. At the main A4069 road turn right for the railway station, less than half a kilometre away. Otherwise turn left for the village and the route through to Llandeilo.

Refreshments and Accommodation

Myddfai: café and visitor centre, plus accommodation
Llangadog: post office and shop, inns and accommodation

Bus and Train

Buses from Llangadog to Llandovery and Llandeilo, service 288/289
Railway halt at Llangadog

Egret at Lougher

13 LLANGADOG STATION TO LLANDEILO STATION

16 km (10 miles)

The trail joins forces with Beacons Way at Llangadog railway station, soon to rise away from the Tywi valley and through the quiet village of Bethlehem. It then climbs up one of the largest fortifications in Wales at Carn Goch, gaunt Iron Age remains exposed to a westerly wind and rain. The trail continues to rise once more to wetter ground at Bwlch-y-Gors, where it passes through Carreglwyd Forest. At Blaen Cib the trail parts company with Beacons Way to descend through wet rush pastures to Coed Tregib and onward across the water meadows of the Tywi into Llandeilo.

Langadog railway station is about half a kilometre from the centre of the village along the A4069 so take care. Leave the station entrance, cross the main road with care and turn right to walk over the railway crossing and along the pavement, as far as the turning before Pont Brân where the pavement gives out. Pass by the church on your left and then up towards the square.

langadog has a square lined with inns and pubs so you'll not die of thirst here. Many of these hostelries would have catered for the drovers passing through to markets in the east of Wales and England. It must have been a little like the wild west when several descended on the township looking for refreshment. Llangadog also had a number of mills powering the making of wool fabric and corn. These mills made good use of the fast flowing Brân and Sawdde rivers. It was also known for its mega creamery situated near to Llangadog railway station, which produced a variety of dairy products, some which were distributed by rail in earlier decades, until the closure of the plant in 2005.

The church of St Cadog lies at the centre of the community, but the remains of the Norman motte and bailey is situated to the south east of Llangadog. It dates from the late 12th century and was ransacked

more than once in the first decade of 13th century. Clearly the locals took a real dislike to its founder Gilbert de Clare, known as Red Gilbert on account of the colour of his hair rather than having a socialist disposition.

2 Be vigilant here, for it is easy to miss your turning! Look for a right turn (No signage in village) along a narrow thoroughfare, just after Llangadog Post Office. This leads to a junction with Walters Road. Go right for about 100 metres along it before turning left onto a path between houses, then continuing ahead between gardens. Pass through a kissing gate into a pasture. Continue ahead through pastures and two more kissing gates onto Carreg Sawdde Common, which is a nature reserve. Go ahead for a few steps, over a footbridge where you come to a junction of paths; keep left here to proceed through scrub. Continue ahead and you'll see a barn on the left in an adjacent field. The path comes out on to the road where you cut right for the bridge across the Afon Sawdde. Alternatively, you might cut across to the Pont Sawdde directly as it is open access land, *at one time a larger unenclosed common, held by the Bishops of St Davids in the late 13th century.*

3 Go over the bridge and keep ahead on the Bethlehem Road into the village of Felindre. Take the second turn right and walk up to another junction. Keep left here along a track between dwellings, and through a field gate into a pasture. Follow the left hand hedge, through another field gate, then go through the kissing gate on the left and turn right to walk alongside a hedge, now to your right, passing through three more kissing gates in fields prior to Bryngwyn Farm. As you near the barn, go ahead through two field gates immediately to the right of it. Proceed along the farm drive, through a kissing gate to a lane and continue ahead again, past another farm on the left, and then eventually arrive at a group of houses at Dolau farm on the right.

4 The lane bends right, but you need to continue ahead at this point. However, do not stay on the track. Make your way through the field gate on the left leading into a hillside pasture. Now follow a bridleway along the fence line on your right at first, rising up alongside a wood to pass through a gateway and a squelchy area. Keep climbing up the hillside to reach a stile by a field gate. Go over it and up again through two small gates before reaching a road. Turn right to make your way along it to Bethlehem where there is an interpretation board and seat to rest awhile.

Bethlehem *derives its name from an early 19th century chapel, which you pass on the way up to Carn Goch. The chapel signalled the revival of Methodism in these parts. The local post office is very popular in the run up to Christmas when people travel from miles around to post their Christmas cards in the village. There's a unique handstamp from Bethlehem and some 30,000 or more greetings cards are sent from this location each year.*

5 Keep ahead at the junction, dropping down to a second junction opposite a bungalow. Go left through a kissing gate next to a field gate, and proceed along a track to come to sheds ahead and dwellings on the left. Continue to the wall at the back of the houses; go left along it for 20 metres and right through a small

63

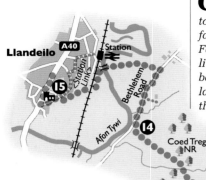

*C*arn Goch *is a defensive site par excellence; the remains are thought to be at least 2500 years old. There are, in fact, two Iron Age hillforts here; Y Gaer Fawr, (the big fort) and Y Gaer Fach, (the little fort) and the stone ramparts can still be seen as you make your way through the larger hillfort which was occupied until the imperial advance of the Roman Army*

gate into a meadow. Head slightly right to pass through a field gate and then follow the hedge to the right as far as Bethlehem chapel. This gives out at a kissing gate on to a lane; go right and gather your strength for a climb up to the car park for Carn Goch about 1.5 km (1 mile) of climbing, situated just off the road.

6 The trail makes its way through this ancient monument, but is not guided by waymark posts, although there is a clear green swathe of grass to follow. The trail peels off left from the car park and bends right to climb up to pass through the indistinct remains of a small ancient Iron Age camp. *On a good day there are splendid panoramic views along this section; somehow if feels different standing where Iron Age people lived for generations.* The path then dips down a little and climbs up again just to the right of a formidable pile of stones; follow the path along them and then cut left to rise up to the inner camp of the main hill fort which is very clear to see. Continue ahead and then very slightly right to the end of the camp where the path eases down gently enough across a heath strewn with stones. It curves slightly right to run down to a lane; the electricity poles present themselves as guide posts.

in approximately AD70. There's something majestic about the place; it is the citadel of forts for most in Wales are far smaller. You'll also pass by a memorial stone to Gwynfor Evans, a long standing MP for Carmarthenshire (Plaid Cymru), who died in 2005. He championed the cause of Welsh language and culture, especially through the medium of a Welsh TV channel.

7 Go right along the lane. Proceed through a field gate at Garn-Wen and walk up the drive for 50 metres, where you cut off slightly left, through a small gate and along a bridleway. The track climbs up to and through another field gate, bends left and right and then you cross a stile to walk ahead again. Rise up to a junction of paths at Bwlch y Gors. Pass through a gate and turn right to follow a path up to another gate and turn right to walk over a boardwalk to a stile, and then slightly right through a gateway. The path then cuts left to follow a fence towards Carreglwyd Woods. *There are lovely views all along this stretch across the Tywi valley.*

8 Go through a gap in a wall, turn right and cross a stile in approximately 60 metres. Now cross another stile and follow a sunken path bordered by gorse and whinberries to a finger post. The path now drops quite steeply to a tractor track. Turn left to climb again through coniferous trees. Continue straight across at the crossroads and then climb a stile onto moorland where you continue ahead with the craggy outcrop of Carn Powell to the left, and

along the drive which bends down left to towards two gates, but beforehand cut left through another field gate. Now follow a track running below the barns; this soon leaves the farm to turn right. You, however, continue ahead through a field gate and follow the hedge to the right along to a stile by a gate.

11 Once over, go slightly left through a field of very lush rush to walk near to the fence to your left. Keep ahead to walk beneath the trees and then proceed ahead for a few paces before cutting slightly right across a second field brimming with common rush. You are aiming for a stile beneath trees part way down; it is not easily seen at first. Cross this stile by a field gate and proceed ahead in the next field to cross a small stream beneath a group of trees. Once through head slightly right across the field to a corner to the right of barns at Llwyn bedw farm. Cross a stile just to the right of a field gate onto a lane.

Coed Tregib has been described, by the outdoor writer Christopher Somerville, *as 'secret and tangled', and so it is. This Woodland Trust wood is well known for its extensive display of bluebells and other flowers in Spring. It is a Site of Special Scientific Interest given the rich diversity of flora, as well as its canopy of ash, oak and alder. Dormice have also been recorded at this site. While it is described as ancient woodland, the site was completely felled in the First World War, although some of*

some streamlets to be crossed before you tackle the ladder stile in the next boundary wall, the first on the trail! Continue ahead along the fence and then strike out across the field to a field gate, which leads to a lonely road junction. *In good weather, you'll catch your first glimpse of the impressive ruins of Castell Carreg Cennen.*

9 Your way is ahead on a road signposted to Trap, continuing along it towards Blaencib and Helgwm woods in about 1 kilometre. *It is a quiet lane offering splendid views across to Carreg Cennen, and you'll pass the turning on the right to Blaen Cib Farm.* Soon after, the Beacons Way leads off left across heathland on route to Castell Carreg Cennen. However, your way to Llandeilo is via Hafod Farm. Look for the next turning on the right indicated by a fingerpost.

10 Follow the farm track down, passing through a field gate by a cattle grid and turning right towards a farmhouse on the right and barns to the left. Continue

older trees survive at the boundary edges. In earlier centuries oaks were felled in the Tywi valley and floated down the river at high water for shipment at Carmarthen.

12 Go right to drop down the lane to a bridge over the Afon Cib and then rise up to pass a group of cottages. The lane bends left by a saw mill at Cib and then pass a turning on the left to Cwm canol. Look for the entrance to Tregib Wood on the right. The path through Coed Tregib is permissive and we are grateful to the Woodland Trust (www.woodlandtrust. org.uk) for allowing access through this splendid woodland.

13 Pass a gap by a gate and descend through the wood. The main path descends to a junction at a waymark post. Go ahead here; the path winds its way between trees curving slightly left and then right down to cross a stream. This is where it gets difficult at present, but be assured that there are improvements in the pipeline. Cross the stream and head slightly right through very muddy ground until you reach a boardwalk. Follow this to exit by a wooden sculpture of an otter. Go ahead, through a gate into younger woodland protected by deer fences. Walk ahead again and then along a compacted path to reach a car park. Cut right here, before the road, on a path leading to a small gate onto Bethlehem Lane.

14 Go right and continue over Pont Breinant, walking along the road; be wary of traffic along this stretch. Look for a footpath signpost on the left, after the entrance to Castell Ddu. The surfaced path leads off left down to a gate and then across a water meadow. *This is your way to a wonderful suspension bridge built in 1911 and known locally as the Swingbridge spanning the Afon Tywi.* The path continues ahead and then left along a corralled section, before joining a track running beneath the railway line and up to Church Street. Turn left here to continue on the trail to Ffairfach, joining the main A483 road. Keep ahead on the pavement, across the Tywi Bridge and ahead to a crossroads in Ffairfach. Turn left here to continue on the trail to Llandybie.

15 Otherwise, if you are visiting Llandeilo, go right and immediately left in Church Street to mosey along Abbey Terrace to the town centre. If you are heading for Llandeilo station then go right along Crescent Road, right into Latimer Road and then right again down Alan Road to cut down a brick surfaced path to Llandeilo Railway Station.

Refreshments and Accommodation

Llandeilo: cafés, shops, restaurants, inns and accommodation

Bus and Train

Buses from Swansea and Ammanford to Llandeilo, service X13 and 103
Buses from Carmarthen and Llandovery to Llandeilo service 288/289
Railway station at Llandeilo

14 LLANDEILO TO AMMANFORD
19 km (11.8 miles)

From either Ffairfach or Llandeilo the trail climbs through the foothills into the western fringe of the Brecon Beacons National Park, a pastoral landscape punctuated with wet rush and marshy woodland. The imposing site of Castell Carreg Cennen is soon in sight; it mesmerising as you walk through fields towards it. The path dips to cross the Cennen before rising to the high ground of Carreg Dwfn, at one time a hotspot of quarrying. The trail passes through the hamlet of Llandyfân and follows a woodland ridge through to the old village of Llandybie. From there follow a heritage trail through pastures to the upper Llwchwr valley and Ammanford.

I From Llandeilo station up platform (for trains in the direction of Shrewsbury and Crewe) walk up steps and then along a path which bends right into the bottom of Alan Road. Turn left to walk up Alan Road until you reach the main A483 road. Go left to walk through the town centre on Rhosmaen Street. The road descends to pass St Teilo's church and proceed ahead to cross the bridge over the Afon Tywi to enter Ffairfach. Go left at the main crossroads into Bethlehem Road.

It is said that Teilo, a 6th century Celtic saint, established a small monastic settlement on the site of the present-day parish church and his association gave the town its name of Llandeilo. The spread of Georgian houses lead to a tight knit pattern of streets from an earlier period. Llandeilo showed defiance to the turbulence of medieval times, but was razed to the ground on several occasions. There's a local walk to Penlan Park where there are superb views from the bandstand across the town. There are also fine views between Llandeilo and Ffairfach on the road bridge over the Afon Tywi which is of historic interest. The single-arched road bridge was completed in 1848 and is Grade II listed. As you cross it you'll also see the railway bridge, opened in 1852, a rare survival of an early 'town-type' lattice girder truss.

Dinefwr Castle is in the hands of the National Trust/CADW and overlooks the River Tywi, about a kilometre and a half to the west of the town lying on a ridge on the northern bank of the Tywi, with a steep drop to the river. Dinefwr was the principal seat of the kingdom of Deheubarth ruled over by Rhys ap Gruffydd in what was known as Welsh kingdoms within Pura Wallia. There is also a deer park, woodland and Newton House to discover. Perhaps most endearing are the ancient oaks to admire as you wander around the park. No wonder then that many an early travel diarist waxed lyrical about Llandeilo and its environs. Llandeilo is a Walkers are Welcome town so that's even better.

2 From Ffairfach railway station, go right at the end of the platform over the crossing, then walk along the other side of the main road to the crossroads. Cross back over to turn right into Bethlehem Road where those starting at Llandeilo will join. *Ffairfach was an important burial site in prehistoric times and, in later centuries for the milling of corn, and other agricultural products. With the coming of the railways it grew in importance, which in turn stimulated local trade in the valley.*

3 Proceed along the pavement and under the rail bridge. Go next right onto the

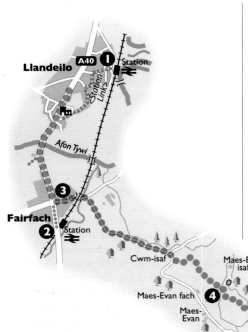

4 Climb over a stile leading into the wood. Press on over another stream to climb a second stile. Head very slightly left through marshy ground towards the next boundary, but don't go through the gate; instead bear to the left of the gate, through a large gap in an old hedge. Step over a small stream here and turn right to walk up ahead to a stile at the top right corner of the field. Once you are over, keep ahead to go over two stiles and a footbridge. Proceed ahead up a large field filled with common wet rush, then cross two stiles in succession at the boundary into the next field. Keep ahead on a path which runs between healthy tufts of grass; continue ahead through a gap, over a stream and up a bank towards Gelli-Groes farm. Go through a field gate and turn right to pass through two more gates; the track leads up to a drive. Go right along it, with cottages on your right, proceeding ahead to a road.

Trap road. This climbs away from the settlement for just under 1 kilometre to Cwm Isaf, where you'll pass by a lane off to the left. About 20 metres up from the junction, go left over a stile then head diagonally right up a pasture to cross a stile by a tree. Walk ahead, with a wall and hedge on the right. Step over a small stream on the right, go up steps and cross another stile. Once over, head up the bank through bracken and damp grassland. It is also overgrown by common rush. Cross a stile beneath an oak tree at the top right hand side of the field. Continue ahead alongside a tree lined boundary, skirting a pocket of woodland. Go ahead to the top right hand corner of this rough pasture to cross a stream although this is very boggy causing locals to go right through a gap and then immediately left across the stream.

5 Turn left and immediately right on the road to cross a stile into a pasture. Follow the hedge on the left down the field. Cross a stile on the left into a pocket of rough ground. Now go ahead to another stile and cross over a green lane to climb a third stile. Head very slightly right across the pasture, proceed through a gap in a wall and then onward to cross the next stile. There is a junction of paths in this field; you will see Penywaun farm over to the left.

6 Head slightly right across another rush pasture, climb a stile at the next boundary and head very slightly right again over another pasture to cross a second stile and a stream. Keep ahead with the hedge to your left. Cross yet another stile and follow the path as it drops down to climb over a stile and stream. Go through the wet ground to stepping stones over a stream, the last on this section. Climb up to a stile, along a green lane, going through a small gate and by Capel Isaac to a junction by Castle View farm. Go right onto the road, turn left but keep right as signposted towards Castell Carreg Cennen.

The imposing location of Castell Carreg Cennen, on limestone cliffs above the Afon Cennen, is best described as inspirational. Historians suggest that it was built in the late 12th century as part of the great Deheubarth dynasty and was fiercely contested by the Welsh and Norman overlords throughout the medieval period. In 1283 Edward I gave the castle to John Giffard, the commander of the English troops at Cilmeri, where Llywelyn ap Gruffudd (The Last) was killed. He made major changes to the old fortification, and the castle, whilst badly dented by constant attacks, resisted the siege of Owain Glyndŵr in 1403. In 1462, during the Wars of the Roses, Castell Carreg Cennen became a Lancastrian stronghold. However, a Yorkist force captured the castle and made a fairly good job of dismantling it. The castle stood in ruins for centuries. It was not until the 19th century that repairs were made in earnest to restore the structure to its admirable state that we see now.

7 At the next junction, go right (unless you are visiting the café or castle, in which case go ahead). This road winds down beneath the castle and bends sharp left to a dwelling at Pantyffynont. Just before, go right down steps, through a gate into a hillside pasture. The path curves right away from the dwelling to cross a stile, then drops down more steeply, where there are steps down to a stile and footbridge over the Afon Cennen.

8 Once over, you head slightly left up a bank, cross a stile in a hedge and then climb up the hillside near to the hedge on your left, curving right to pass beneath Llwyn-bedw. Join a track to the right of the dwelling and keep ahead along it to Nant Llygad Llwchwr where you cross a footbridge. Continue along the main track, ignoring paths off to the left. The track curves around to the right to Cwrtbrynbeirdd, where it bends sharp left before the farmhouse, *said to have been a court housing bards associated with Carreg Cennen in earlier centuries. Robert Macfarlane in The Old Ways muses that we should look to the histories of a route and its previous followers. It makes you wonder how many bards have trodden this path in past times!* The track eventually gives out on to a road.

9 Turn left to walk by the entrance to an old quarry on the right, for this is an area where several limestone ridges have been worked. *The entrance to a bottled water producer is on the left.* As the road begins to bend to the left, keep right over a cattle grid and up a track, passing by a number of dwellings. At the junction turn right to climb up on a track onto Carreg Dwfn. This bends to the left. You soon pass by some old buildings in an adjacent field, and the track descends down the open access land to more buildings on the right known as Cefn Coed Isaf .

69

10 At this point, go over a stile on the right and turn left and walk ahead through the next pasture to reach a stile. Cross this and follow the path down rough pasture to buildings at Pant Glas. Continue ahead along the lane to reach Llandyfân where the church of St Dyfan is on the right, *a Grade II listed building where Ffynnon Gwyddfân attracted many pilgrims in earlier centuries seeking restorative cures for their ailments.*

11 Cross over the road and head slightly right to go through a small gate into a field. Go ahead by an electricity pole and then drop down the field to a small gate below. Continue ahead on a boardwalk over rocky and muddy ground and then head across wet ground aiming slightly left to a kissing gate to enter a wood. Go right and follow the path which bends left and right near to an old boundary wall. This leads up to a small gate.

12 Exit onto the road and turn right to walk down the bank, but be sure to cross over before the bend. Go left on the track through a kissing gate by a field gate and then pass by an old limestone works. Keep ahead at a junction and ahead again through a kissing gate by a field gate. The path climbs up left between brambles into a meadow and continues ahead through a large gap in the hedge. Go ahead to proceed through a kissing gate in the next boundary. Once through, look for a kissing gate on the left leading into the wood. The path cuts right down through the wood making your way through patches of bracken and brambles to a fence. Go through a gate and continue ahead as the path winds its way to a small gate which you pass through, before curving left and right to another small gate. Go through it and head slightly left down to a stile by a gate.

13 Cross it and walk along a grassy path above at garden at Pistyll-bâch. Pass by an old garden building to cross a stile and another through rough ground to cross another. The way is not entirely clear here as there has been a change of route from the old line of path. Please note that there is currently a diversion order in place and if successful these instructions will be superseded by new waymarks indicating a new route. Until the diversion is in place it is best to make your way ahead by the old oaks trees, as waymarked, and then slightly left up the hillside on a track to the brow of the hill. You will now encounter horses, and where there have been continued use of electric fences to coral them, so be careful as you duck and dive through to a kissing gate located by a field gate between the stables. This exits onto a road.

Station
Llandybie

14 Go right to walk down the road to Llandybie railway station and village centre, a few minutes beyond, where there is a café, shops and inns as well as the bus stops for Ammanford and Llandeilo on the main road. If you are continuing to Ammanford do not go as far as the railway crossing; go left along an unmarked road between older houses on the left. If you see Erw'r Brenhindedd on the left you have just missed the turning; there's no fingerpost here so it is easily done!

15 If starting at Llandybie railway station, turn right over the crossing and pass by a turning for housing at Erw'r Brenhindedd. Turn next right along an unmarked track between older houses. Proceed through a small gate next to a field gate leading into a paddock. Go right. Before reaching the hedge and field gate, cut left through a small gate to climb up

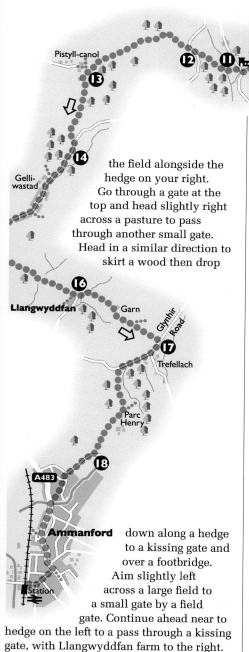

the field alongside the hedge on your right. Go through a gate at the top and head slightly right across a pasture to pass through another small gate. Head in a similar direction to skirt a wood then drop

down along a hedge to a kissing gate and over a footbridge. Aim slightly left across a large field to a small gate by a field gate. Continue ahead near to hedge on the left to a pass through a kissing gate, with Llangwyddfan farm to the right.

16 Continue ahead for several metres then cut left over a footbridge. Turn right to go along the track to meet a lane. Go left along it for about 60-70 metres. Make sure you keep right at the fork, through a small gate by a cattle grid and up the drive towards a house. By the house, you will see a kissing gate on the right hand side leading into an adjacent field. This is your way. Once through the gate, climb up alongside the hedge to your left, passing a pocket of trees at the top. The path curves right to two gates on the left in a thick hedge. Go through them and then turn right along a green track for about 10 metres, left through a kissing gate and onward to reach a small gate. Keep ahead now with a hedge to the right to a field boundary and proceed again in the next field to a kissing gate leading onto Glynhir Road.

17 Turn right and follow the Glynhir Road past a turning on the left. Continue ahead here and before the road bends right go left, through a kissing gate by a field gate down a track towards Parc Henry. The track descends a field, through two kissing gates and drops down to the next boundary where it bends right, through a gate by a field gate and then left and right to continue downhill through another to Parc Henry Road.

18 Keep right here and, as the lane bends right through the housing development, turn left by the fingerpost, down steps and between gardens. Cross a road and continue ahead on a similar path to reach the main road at Bonllwyn. Go left to walk along the green, and then onward towards the town, a good ten minute walk from here. If you are for Ammanford railway station go right along Station Road and third right. Otherwise continue on the Llandybie Road into the town centre; the bus station is on the left.

Refreshments and Accommodation

Ffairfach: inns and accommodation

Castell Carreg Cennen: café

Trap: one kilometre from the trail, inn and accommodation

Llandybie: café, restaurant, inns and a general store

Glynhir: half a kilometre from the trail, accommodation

Ammanford: cafés, shops, restaurants, inns and accommodation

Bus and Train

Buses from Llandeilo to Llandybie and Ammanford, service X13 and 103

Buses from Llandybie to Ammanford, service X13, 103 164/165

Railway halts at Llandybie and Ammanford

15 AMMANFORD STATION TO PONTARDDULAIS STATION

14 km (8.7 miles)

The trail crossesthe Afon Aman to rise up the slopes of Garnswllt and onto Graig Fawr, a long heathland ridge with wet flushes, a place that feels distinctly remote and with exceptional views across to the Gower peninsula. It descends into Pontarddulais, a small town, at one time known for its production of tinplate.

Leave Ammanford railway station, turn right into Station Road and left at the main junction. Turn right into College Street (A483) to walk through town, passing the bus station on the left, to the junction corralled by pedestrian railings. Cross the road to proceed ahead along Quay Street, a pedestrianised area which leads to a sculpture by Howard Bowcott, depicting the mining heritage of the town. Go ahead again at the first roundabout, passing by the Railway Hotel, and through gates over the Amman Valley railway line. Continue to another roundabout and aim towards the Park Street bridge over the Afon Aman. However, go right immediately before the bridge on a surfaced path alongside the river. Follow this down to the rear of Tesco supermarket, where you cut right across a road (currently a dead end) to join the walking and cycling route to Pantyffynnon, which also happens to be the Fair Trade Way at this point. This runs along the back of the supermarket, then left alongside security fencing and the railway track.

*A*mmanford *(Rhydaman) was originally named Cross Inn, after one of the town's coaching inns. It remained as a major crossroads on the north-south and east-west coach routes in the early 19th century. However, in 1880 the good and great of the town decided to re-name it as Ammanford. Coal was mined extensively in the 19th century which attracted a considerable migration of workers. This included several Italian families who established a reputation for fine coffee and ice cream parlours.*

Additional investment led to various companies, one of which was the Llanelly Railway and Dock Company, to build a railway up from the coast. It opened in 1840, linking Llanelli through to Brynamman by 1842 and later extending northwards to Llandeilo and beyond. The

signal box at Pantyfynnon is a Grade II listed building dating from the late 1880s and the railway buildings, also Grade II listed have been beautifully restored in recent years winning a Railway Heritage Trust Conservation award.

2 You now reach a junction. For those finishing a walk at Pantyffynnon railway station, go over the tracks again and turn left for the station, about 5 minutes at most. Otherwise, go left at the junction to continue. If you are starting your walk at Pantyffynon railway station, leave the platform by the crossing and go right along Pantyffynon Road. Look for a road off to the right across the railway line, and keep ahead to join the main route.

3 The path runs alongside Pantyfynnon rugby club ground to cross a suspension bridge over the Afon Aman, and a small footbridge over a tributary stream. Follow the tarmac lane up to the village of Garnswllt, where you come to a turning circle and houses. Go left to walk up the road, Lon y Felin, through a housing estate to a junction with Heol y Garn. Turn right here and pass by a row of houses to your right. As the road bends right, go left along a track past two more houses then, through a metal gate to a wooded slope where there were once quarry workings.

4 Now look for a path up steps through the wood (also waymarked as Penlle'r Castell Walk). Climb more steps through the old workings and even more to reach a stile into a field so you'll probably need a breather here. With the old boundary wall on the left, covered with grass and moss, continue straight ahead up the slopes of Garnswllt until joining a tree line wall running at right angles. Go right along the wall for about 10-15 metres and then cut left over a stile. Continue straight ahead uphill, keeping a ruined wall and

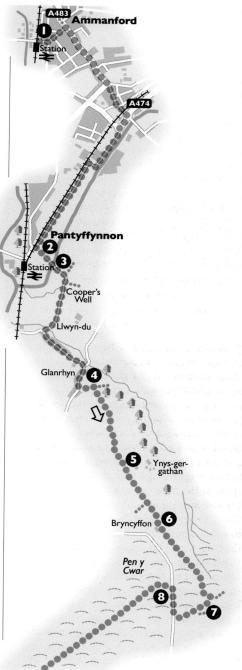

hawthorns on your right, until after about 100 metres you encounter another wall coming in from the left. The two walls then channel you firstly to the right, then to the left, where there is a solitary waymark post indicating a direction uphill. Continue to climb, heading diagonally up the hillside to a narrow gate nestled by a field gate. Once through, keep ahead with a fence to the right to a go through a kissing gate.

5 Cross a farm track and pass through another kissing gate to climb again with a fence now on the left rising up to a few steps and a small gate. Once through, keep ahead again across a pasture, through another gate by a field gate, and onward to reach a stile in a wooden fence. Cross a stile and keep slightly right to pass through a wooden field gate to reach the bucolic ruins of Bryncyffon farm.

6 Walk by the ruins and through a small gate in a field gate. Proceed through another small gate and continue alongside woodland and fencing to rise up the valley along a green track in the same south-easterly direction. Continue to rise as it edges up the valley towards a line of pylons on the skyline; you are aiming to the right of the right hand pylon. You'll pass through wet ground as the track becomes rougher, curving slightly left until you meet a track coming up from the left, St Illtyd's Walk, which you join for the walk through to Pontarddulais.

7 Go right onto this farm track which curves slightly left up to join a wider track. Go right here to walk alongside it to a public highway where you turn right again and rise gently uphill. When this road begins to descend look for two tracks leading off left (this route is now different to the St Illtyd's Walk shown on older OS maps).

8 Keep ahead on the left hand green track, which bends left and right then peters out as you proceed across the moor. Continue ahead, aiming for a waymark post to assist navigation, across the expanse of heathland known as Graig Fawr (the compass bearing in poor visibility is 240°). Continue ahead, now rising slowly towards another waymark post on the horizon; there are tracks along this section, wet in winter, but often dry as a bone in summer, often used by horse riders and farm vehicles. This dips slightly at first then rises again, bending slightly right and then left to pass to the right of a triangulation point. *On reaching the higher ground, you'll soon capture wonderful views of the Llwchwr Estuary and the Gower Peninsula beyond, Swansea, and Port Talbot to the south east and in the west are the Preseli Mountains.*

G raig Fawr is primarily open moorland covered in heath grass and wavy hair grass, heather and bilberry. You'll more than likely see a brown hare if it is quiet. There are also pockets of bog where cotton grass grows. In a wetter part of the moor there are rare varieties of sphagnum moss growing, harvested here in earlier times for use in dressing war wounds, given its absorbent and mildly antiseptic properties. You might also see low level upright stones near to the trail, some of the many prehistoric sites which are located on the moor. They are Neolithic burial chambers and historians suggest that some may possibly be the foundations of early dwellings.

Pontarddulais

9 From the triangulation point, continue ahead along the plateau to pick up a track, (the compass bearing for poor visibility is 220 degrees). This track, faint at first, soon becomes

increasingly more defined. You will soon be able to see the tapestry of fields and pockets of woodland to the right in the Loughor Valley. Follow the waymark posts as the track descends gently at first then more steeply as it cuts right and then left down a slope; there are outcrops to the left. Follow the main track as it ventures across the bracken clad moor, with other tracks joining from time to time. You eventually drop down to a metal gate and a bungalow beyond, to leave the moorland at Pentrebach.

10 Follow the lane ahead as it passes by a number of dwellings down to a junction. Turn right here to walk along a steep sided lane of some antiquity, bordered by a line of beautiful old oak trees. It passes through an urban area, along Dantwyn Road, to a junction by a green. Go left along Glynhir Road and then this continues into Caecerrig Road, past a school, and onto Dulais Road, where there is a bus stop for Swansea on the left. Follow Dulais Road to a junction with St Teilo's Street. Turn right here to pass through the centre of town to a junction. Go right for the main bus stops (and public toilets), or keep ahead for Pontarddulais railway station, which is signposted off to the right before the bridge over the Afon Llwchwr. The traffic light junction marks the site of where the closed section of the Central Wales line from Pontarddulais to Swansea Victoria crossed the road on the level

Refreshments and Accommodation
Pontarddulais: cafés, shops, restaurants, inns and accommodation

Bus and Train
Buses from Swansea to Pontarddulais and Ammanford service X13
Buses from Llanelli to Pontarddulais.L3 and L4
Railway halt at Pontarddulais

16 PONTARDDULAIS STATION TO BYNEA STATION
via Morfa Mawr
10 km (6 miles)
or via Llangennech
10 km (6 miles)
and then onward to LLANELLI STATION
*10 km (6 miles), **a total of 20 km (12 miles)***

There are two routes available south of Pontarddulais, as east of the Llwchwr can flood at high tide, making the trail impassable at Morfa Mawr. It is possible to check the tidal range at www.willyweather.co.uk/wl/carmartheshire/river-loughor-entrance.html
If the tidal range is high when you want to walk then it might be best to select the Western Route via Llangennech. This follows a route above the western side of the Llwchwr Estuary and is not affected by tidal water. Either way, the routes meet in Bynea ready to join the Wales Coast Path through to Llanelli

EAST ROUTE via MORFA MAWR (when the tide is low)

*T*he name **Pontarddulais** refers to an earlier bridge over the Afon Llwchwr which is long since gone, but the old nickname remains for locals call the town Bont (meaning bridge) for short. In past times it was famous for its production of tinplate and now it is known for the numerous bridal shops around town. The Railway Station was opened in 1839, as part of the Llanelly Railway (original spelling) which was purpose built for use by steam locomotives. Pontarddulais railway station eventually developed into an imposing junction for that line, and the later LNWR line from Swansea Victoria via Dunvant and Gorseinon, when it opened in 1867. From that date, Swansea Victoria continued to serve as the southern terminus for the Heart of Wales line until 1964, when this scenic portion of the line which ran along Swansea Bay and up the Clyne Valley, was closed.

*T*he **Beca Stone** commemorates the site of a turnpike tollgate in Pontarddulais which was destroyed in the Rebecca Riots. The riots were a series of violent protests by farmers and agricultural workers (often dressed as women, hence the name) against what was considered to be unfair rents, taxation and worsening economic conditions of the time. They took place between 1839 and 1843 in South and Mid Wales targeting tollgates as the roadbuilders were seen as the least reasonable in terms of rents and tolls charged.

1 From Pontarddulais railway station, turn left onto the main road (A48), ahead at the crossroads and cross over at pedestrian crossing. Go left along the pavement and right into St Teilo Street through the town centre. At the Farmers Arms, turn next right into Trinity Place and then, within 50 metres left at the fork into Coed Bach. This leads into Coed Bach Park.

2 Continue ahead on the main path but, when it bends right, go down for about 20 metres and then left alongside a sports pitch. At the end of the pitch, turn right and then left to proceed through a kissing gate, over a footbridge and across the line of the old Central Wales line from Pontarddulais to Swansea Victoria. Proceed to another kissing gate. Here there is a junction of paths signposted. Do not take the path signposted left which rises slightly uphill, nor follow a track which drops slightly right and downhill to a double field gate. Instead go straight ahead towards a hedge, in which a kissing gate is concealed. This kissing gate leads onto a hard-surfaced footpath to the banks of the Afon Llwchwr.

3 Follow this hard-surfaced path and on reaching the riverside, go left to cross a footbridge. Proceed through a kissing gate and continue alongside the river bank. Cross another footbridge and through a kissing gate and then with the fence to the right, proceed through another three kissing gates aiming towards the farm buildings ahead. Here there is a junction of paths. *Ahead in the saltings, lies the graveyard of the former church of Llandeilo Talybont, famous for its mediaeval wall-paintings, which was dismantled stone by stone and has now been re-erected in the Welsh Folk Museum at St Fagans. This short diversion of 200 metres is well-worth the effort.* Otherwise, turn left through a kissing gate and pass round the outside of the farm buildings to join the farm access track.

Go through a kissing gate near to the farm and turn left along this track towards the motorway.

4 Pass beneath the motorway, through a field gate and then follow the track as it firstly bends left and then to the right. *You might be able to catch a glimpse here of the mound of a 12th century motte and bailey castle which guarded an early river crossing hereabouts.* Walk under the railway and continue ahead. Cross the bridge over a stream by Castell-Ddu, then go right to cross a stile by a gate. Follow the track as it bends left and becomes a path with the estuary to the right; you can smell the sea air! Cross a stile and continue ahead and slightly left to a stile in a fence, 80 metres distant, crossing over a stream by a railway sleeper-type footbridge and a track. Cross a stile into a field and then walk with the fence to your right through a wet patch to a stile step. Cross this and continue ahead in the next field. Climb a stone step stile and proceed slightly left to a second stone step stile. Once over, continue to walk very slightly right to a third stone stile. Finally drop down slightly right to a wooden stile and small bridge to a road by Grove Farm.

5 Go left on the road for about 10-15 metres to turn right through a gate and rise up to another gate. Pass through and follow the field hedge to your right to walk up the field, soon curving right into marshy ground. *Warning – this particular section can become a quagmire in wet weather.* Aim for the very top left hand corner, as the field narrows, where there's a stile beneath bushes. Cross it and the small bridge to enter the next field. Turn left to walk alongside the hedge on your left. You reach a kissing gate on the left. Go through and then aim slightly right. Cross the stile near to the gate and walk along the hedge on the right. You come to a kissing gate just beyond a track, and once through, continue ahead to another stile by a field gate. Proceed with a fence to the right to cross a stile in the corner a few metres right of a field gate. Turn left and then right, to walk along a track leading by a house to reach Llannant Road.

6 Cross over and proceed through a kissing gate opposite into a field. Head slightly left to a second kissing gate and continue ahead with a hedge and housing to the left. Cross a stile by a gate and continue along a path. Cross another stile by a second gate and continue ahead to cross a third stile along a green way. Now follow the track ahead through a gate, soon crossing another stile by a gate. This leads to a junction with Gwyn-faen farm across to the right. Go left for 100 metres or so.

7 Go through a kissing gate and turn right along Gwynfe Road which bends right and then left. Continue along it to reach more dwellings, but before the main car park you will see a fingerpost on the right. Follow the path here which curves. left, as indicated by waymarks, and then as it bends back right to go out to the point, just as you reach the car park, keep ahead to join a path along the foreshore of the Llwchwr towards some factory buildings in the distance. Leave the park by a gate and ahead on a road by a factory and Loughor Boating Club then along the pavement to the Loughor Bridge.

8 Go right to cross the bridge, which can be blustery and the traffic scary. At the far end of the bridge turn right to descend steps and go ahead towards the Schaeffler factory. At the junction, turn left to walk along Yspitty Road. Those wishing to go

to Bynea railway station should continue ahead for a 10 minute walk to the station located on the right. Otherwise, go left to cross over the B4297 to join the Wales Coast Path, through a car park and to a junction. Go left here.

L oughor Castle is a short diversion from the trail. Just before reaching the Loughor Bridge, turn left by a small car park. Walk up the bank on Ferry Road. After 100 metres you reach the A4240, the main road through the village of Loughor, which is also the route of the Wales Coast path at this point. The castle mound and ruins of Loughor castle are ahead. There's an information board about the castle and the Roman fort which preceded the castle on this site. To continue your journey, return to the A4240 and follow the Coast Path signs to Loughor Bridge. The abutments on your right are the remains of an earlier 1923 road bridge which replaced a treacherous river crossing, which could only be forded at very low tide.

As you cross the bridge, you will note the new railway bridge on your left, which carries the main South Wales railway linking Swansea to Llanelli and West Wales. It was opened in 2013, but incorporates some earlier sections of the preceding viaduct. A plaque situated halfway across and on the seaward side of the road bridge, describes the project and its construction. Whilst, at the far end of the bridge, again on the seaward side, there is a section of the original 1852 Brunel railway viaduct, as modified in 1909, which was removed and put on display by Network Rail when the new railway crossing over the Llwchwr was opened.

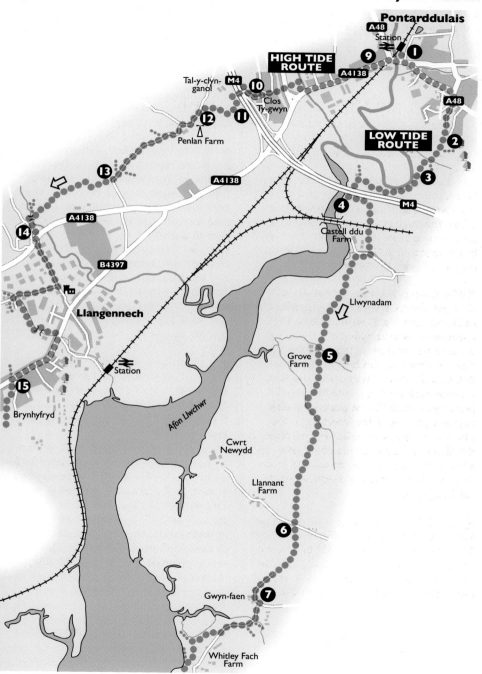

WEST ROUTE VIA LLANGENNECH
(when the tide is high)

9 The trail partly follows the route of St Illtyd's Walk through to Penlan Farm, though it does manage to avoid some of the main road walking by using Hendy Park. Proceed from Pontarddulais railway station to the main road and turn right to walk up to the mini roundabout. Cross over to pass by the Black Horse Inn and ahead along Iscoed Road towards Hendy.

10 Clos Ty-gwyn bends right and then left. Look for a garage on the right and the trail passes to the rear of this to a kissing gate. Once through, follow the corralled path along the side of a motorway and over the footbridge. It then proceeds to a kissing gate leading into a field, where you can breathe a sigh of relief as you escape the urban fringe.

11 Walk up the field with a hedge to the right. *As you climb up you will see the railway viaduct of the Swansea District line crossing the Llwchwr estuary from this vantage point.* At the top of the field, go through a kissing gate and turn right to go through the next gate into the cemetery. Follow the path up to the lane by Hen Gapel Independent Chapel, dating from the early 18th century, but with some alterations since.

After approximately 500 metres on the main road, turn right into Sawel Road, Past Libanus Chapel, then left into River Terrace, which leads to a bridge over the Afon Gwili and into Hendy Park. Continue ahead through the park to exit into Heol-y-parc, B4306. Cross the road and head up a ginnel which exits onto Heol Llwynbedw. Continue ahead into Ty-gwyn.

12 Go left along the lane until you reach a fork in the road. This is where you part company with St Illtyd's Walk. Keep left at the junction along a winding lane, with celandine, primrose, ferns and bracken adorning its banks. This descends to pass a turning for Tyreglwys Farm on the right and a dwelling on the left. At the next corner leave the road over a stone step stile by a gate into a field.

13 Continue ahead along a track to go through a kissing gate by a field gate in the next boundary, and keep ahead to go through another kissing gate in the next field. Go right to the top field corner then left down to a pocket of mature trees where you cut slightly left to climb a stone stile. In the next field, walk ahead towards the houses and cross a footbridge over the Afon Morlais. The path is corralled through to a road.

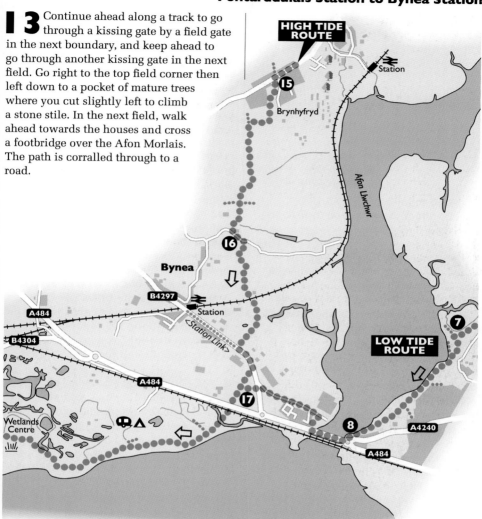

*L*langennech *lies on the western fringe of the Llwchwr estuary. It witnessed rapid growth during the early industrial period. As elsewhere, the development of the village between 1780 and 1850 was at its height when landowners decided to exploit coal reserves here. The coal was duly transported by the Llanelly Dock Railway to the new harbours in Llanelli*

ready for export. The poor suffered changing economic circumstances at this time and the Rebecca Riots spread to the village too in 1843. The Rebecca Daughters visited the Bridge End Toll gate one night to make their point of view known. They completely removed the gate and destroyed part of the toll house as a demonstration of their frustration with heavy toll charges.

14 Cross over the road and turn left to follow the pavement down to a subway which tunnels under the A4183. Continue along Troserch Road to pass a Bethesda Chapel, then turn right into Heol Mwrwg. Follow Mwrwg Road through to a stream, Nant Mwrwg, and go left along the path as signposted through to Bridge Street, the main street in the village of Llangennech. *Those wishing to join a train at Llangennech should continue ahead to cross Bridge Street into Station Road.* To continue on the trail turn right to follow the B4297 uphill on Hendre Road until reaching Brynhyfryd Road on the left, just after a bus shelter.

15 Go along Brynhyfryd Road for approximately 50 metres, then cut right along a bridleway behind gardens. This leads into Pencoed Road where you turn right. The road then bends to the left and as it curves left keep ahead along a corralled path onto a track. Go right to climb up the field to another track. Go left here to walk beneath the buildings at Plas Penlan. The track runs along the field edge, leading down to a kissing gate. Once through continue ahead in the next pasture to a second kissing gate and ahead again to a third gate on a narrow surfaced path. Follow the hedge down to a kissing gate by a field gate. Go right for a few steps and then turn left to follow a hedge down to and through a kissing gate, which is located in a very muddy patch. Aim slightly right across the field towards a kissing gate in the far left hand corner. Go through it and continue ahead to proceed through a final kissing gate onto a lane.

16 Go left along Pencoed-isaf Road and this drops down to a corner look for a kissing gate on the right leading into a field. Follow the hedge which curves around to a more clearly defined track by old works. Follow this down to

Ffos fach, where you need to cross over the railway tracks with care. Continue to follows the track through reed infused pools en route to the main road at Bynea, an area known for its steel and tinplate production. At the main road turn right for Bynea railway station and left to join the Wales Coast Path into Llanelli . By turning left, and proceeding along the B4297, past Huntsman chemical works, the shortest route is to then turn right, immediately after Harry Phillips Car Showroom, along a footpath which joins the Wales Coast Path as it exits the Bynea Gate car park, keep left.

Station Link

From Bynea Station walk up from the platform to Heol-y-Bwlc. Cross the road and continue towards Loughor. Pass the Harry Phillips Showroom on the right which is opposite a chemical works. Look for a concrete track on the right between buildings and a security fence. Go right along it to join the main route coming in from the Bynea Gate car park; continue ahead.

17 Turn first right to walk over the suspension bridge. Continue on the wide track which descends to run alongside the Loughor estuary (shared with cyclists on the Celtic Trail). *Over ten miles of coastline has been developed as the Coastal Millennium Park and this is an exceptional traffic free route through to Pembrey; you can expect to see far more people on this section of route than elsewhere. on the Heart of Wales Line Trail. There are particularly good views across the estuary to Pen-clawdd and the Gower Peninsula. The surface is sometimes compacted and in other places a sealed surface; there are also braids along the seawalls which offer closer views of the seafront.*

18 You eventually reach the entrance to the *Llanelli Wetlands Centre (run by the Wildfowl and Wetlands Trust)* on

Capel Newydd, Hendy

your left, a superb nature reserve which *explains the importance of wetlands and the wildlife which live therein.* If you are not visiting, then cross the road and continue ahead. Before reaching another road go left (signposted Route 4 again) and follow the track as it bends left then right to skirt a golf course. There are parallel paths easing off the main track if you prefer these to get a closer view of the birdlife in the salt marshes.

19 The track eventually comes to an urban development at Machynys, turns right and by the Millennium Beacon joins a road alongside housing. *The area has been rebuilt in recent decades with houses overlooking the sea where* industry was once dominant; brickworks *and tinplate were especially important.* It then turns right again, when it reaches the former entrance channel to the old Copperworks Dock. Follow this to the road and then go left taking the path alongside the road bridge and the roundabout. The track continues alongside a place called Seaside and The Flats where there was considerable development of iron and copper works. *The marshy estuary to the left was the main channel to the Carmarthenshire and North Docks. The Discovery Centre is situated to the west of these waterfronts.* Simply follow the trail as far as the next roundabout to reach it. At that point keep left for the Discovery Centre.

The Coastal Park Discovery Centre is the penultimate call on the trail. It is an iconic Centre situated at the heart of the Coastal Park where are many different habitats, including sand dune, lake, salt marsh, fen, woodland, stream and semi-natural grassland. You may see small flocks of dunlin, ringed plover, sanderling and redshank along the coast whilst shelduck, oystercatcher and curlew can be seen further out on the mudflats. Dock Dunes Local Nature Reserve, next to the Discovery Centre, is home to many specialist plants that are adapted to withstand the dry sandy condition such as sea holly, sea campion, and sea spurge.

Llanelli derives its name from the 7th century saint, St Ellyw. It remained an isolated community until the rapid industrialisation of the 18th and 19th centuries. Two early entrepreneurs A Raby and C Nevill developed the waterfront of the Afon Lliedi so as to ship out coal, and following this initial investment the Carmarthenshire Dock was developed in the last years of the 18th century. In the 19th century iron, steel and tinplate manufacture became dominant and that earned the town the nick-name of Tinopolis (there's a book by John Edwards which explains the town's industrial development in detail). The North Dock was a latecomer, being built in 1904, and the award winning restaurant Sosban is located in the restored pump house.

If you visit the town centre then call into Llanelly House, a lovingly restored Georgian property revitalised in recent years by the Carmarthenshire Heritage Trust. North of the town is Parc Howard, a museum housed in the Italianate mansion of 1885 offering an insight into some of the towns former industries; it is surrounded by extensive park land. Championed by a local group, the Parc Howard Association, this is an exceptional asset for the town. Both properties were donated to the town by industrial magnates, the Stepneys, involved in the town for over two centuries. The Llanelli History Society and Llanelli Community Heritage continue to unravel aspects of the town's heritage whether referring to nonconformist chapels, industrial development or social change and this makes for fascinating reading.

20 If you are not going to call into the Discovery Centre, cross the road on the right before the roundabout and then keep right to walk into Stryd y Mor (Marine Street). Follow this until you reach Glanmor Road easily identified by two historic chapels located nearby. *The Bethel Baptist Chapel and the Siolah Independent Chapels both date from 1840; the former was enlarged in 1850. Llanelli, like many of the rapidly expanding industrial areas of South Wales, has a large number of non-conformist chapels from this period which have served the local population since then, but also give character to many local neighbourhoods.* Go left along Glanmor Road to the crossing gates. Once over the tracks turn right into Great Western Crescent and the entrance to Llanelli station is on the right.

Refreshments and Accommodation

Loughor: shops, inns and accommodation
Llangennech: shops, inns and accommodation
Bynea: inns
Discovery centre, Llanelli: café
Llanelli: shops, inns and accommodation

Bus and Train

Loughor: Buses from Swansea and Llanelli, service XII
Llangennech: Buses from Llanelli and Pontarddulais, service L3 and L4
Railway halts at Llangennech and Bynea